THE
PLAYBOOK

USING SPORTS TO
Unlock Faith Principles

RICKEY FONDREN

FOREWORD BY DR. ELI MORRIS

LUCIDBOOKS

*To my beautiful wife Reagan,
our precious children Rickey III (Trey) and Ryane,
my loving family and supportive friends,
and the entire sports community.*

TABLE OF CONTENTS

FOREWORD

In 2020, I wrote a letter to my former high school track coach upon his retirement from teaching and coaching. I thanked him for his investment years ago in an awkward seventeen-year-old mediocre basketball player he thought might become an awkward seventeen-year-old mediocre high jumper. In my letter, I outlined how God used him to enrich and instruct my life in so many ways.

In *The Playbook,* Rickey Fondren so beautifully reminds us of God's work in our lives through the vehicle of sports. Winning, losing, pushing, competing, training, being a team, overcoming, and recovering are all things I learned about in sports and things I face every day as a Jesus follower. Thank you, Rickey, for creatively weaving the two together!

Sports Credentials: High jumper at Overton High; men's track and field coach at Fairley High (1977–78); high jump coach at Melrose, Whitehaven, and Central High (1979–83); and six marathons. Ran in six marathons and all fifty states for a total of 25,000 miles.

Dr. Eli Morris, Sr. Associate Pastor,
Hope Church, Memphis, Tennessee

JERSEYS IN THE RAFTERS

To my beloved Sports Community: Finally, a play has been drawn up that enables us to look up at the game we fell in love with through the eyes of principle. In *The Playbook*, you will find ample evidence that sports involve so much more than shooting a basketball or throwing a football: sports save lives. You don't have to take my word for it, but I triple-double dare you to ask anybody who has ever played sports about the impact on their life.

The following are testimonials of how basketball, in superhero fashion, has come to the rescue of so many. It's Larry Bird; it's Kenny "The Jet" Smith! It's basketball, . . . and it's coming right at you powered like a locomotive, faster than a speeding bullet to save the day!

Penny Hardaway, NBA Great and Head Coach (Memphis Tigers)

As I began my coaching career at my alma mater, many people were concerned about me ruining my legacy. For me, I'm too concerned with making a difference and helping these kids to be concerned about ruining my legacy. Who better to teach them how to create a culture of sacrifice and challenge them to understand the game from both the mental side and the physical side? After all, you need to be able to play smart along with playing hard. You need to be able to do all of the little things consistently and give multiple efforts. You need to approach the game with the understanding that it teaches you a lot of lessons about life. Lessons like accountability, loyalty, hard work, and dedication; lessons that mold you from being a boy to becoming a man.[1]

Destinee Wells, Guard for the Lady Tennessee Volunteers

Basketball has taught me to go after my dreams and to never allow the opinions of others define who I am![2]

Sports Credentials: Ohio Valley Conference Freshman of the Year, First Team All-OVC (2x), OVC Tournament MVP (2x), OVC All-Tournament Team (2x), Tennessee Sports Writers Association Player of the Year, 2023 Nancy Lieberman Award Watch List. Starred for the Belmont Bruins.

---

[1] "All the Smoke," *The Harder Way*, created by Lebron James, season 1, episode 1, UNINTERRUPTED and ESPN+, in partnership with OBB Pictures, 2020.
[2] Personal communication with the author.

Chris Franklin, Marketing Director at ABC24/CW30 Memphis

> Practice doesn't make perfect; it makes progress. What I haven't prepared for will reveal itself in the game, and the game will reveal what I need to practice. Practice doesn't make perfect; it makes progress. It's a cycle . . . the cycle of life.[3]

Sports Credentials: Played basketball at Fisk University, helping the team to a 17–9 season in 2000.

Mallory Collier, Center for the NC State Lady Wolfpack

> The greatest life lesson that I have learned through sports is to always be obsessed with your own potential! Even if you feel like you can't achieve something, you have to push through and trust the process. In sports, you have to always remain teachable and take feedback in a constructive way, keeping a positive mindset through it all.[4]

Sports Credentials: ESPN #55 Ranked Player c/o 23, 2022 All-Metro Girls Basketball First Team, Nominee for Miss Tennessee Basketball Award, Tennessee Gatorade Player of the Year.

---

[3] Personal communication with the author.
[4] Personal communication with the author.

Ricky Ransom, High School Basketball Guard (MUS Owls class of 2022)

I've learned that mental toughness isn't something one has or doesn't have; it is a skill developed. I see missed shots, turnovers, and errors simply as data—information to help me become better, not as reasons to hang my head. This perspective has had the greatest impact on my confidence as it keeps me steady and out of my head when it's game time. It's only data.[5]

Terry Tippett, Legendary High School Basketball Coach

As a high school basketball coach for nearly fifty years, I have coached tons of mega-talented players; however, I attribute the pinnacle of my success to establishing a team-first culture. There have been players who've come through our program that maybe wanted to shoot more or to be the team's primary playmaker in an effort to build their stock for the next level. And they were allowed to do just that . . . at another school. Far beyond all of the wins and the multiple state championships, the greatest lesson that we've taught through the tool of basketball is that when you identify and embrace culture, you will establish a path to success.[6]

---

[5] Personal communication with the author.
[6] Personal communication with the author.

4

Sports Credentials: Over 900 wins, six-time Tennessee Secondary School Athletic Association (TSSAA) State Champion (Trezevant, White Station, ECS), TSSAA Hall of Fame, Basketball Coaches Association of Tennessee (BCAT) Hall of Fame, multiple-time Coach of the Year.

Dr. Earle Fisher, Sr. Pastor, Abyssinian Missionary Baptist Church, Memphis, TN

> The greatest life lesson that sports taught me is that there are rules and regulations that have to be followed in order to win. Sure, you can master certain strategies and habits that improve your chances for success. But when you fail to master the fundamentals, those chances diminish quickly.[7]

Sports Credentials: Played Basketball at Lemoyne-Owen College, helping them to a Southern Intercollegiate Athletic Conference (SIAC) title in 2000.

Tay Curry, Founder of Lyfestyle Rekreations

> As a kid growing up in the south side of Chicago, you had three choices. You either gang bang, become a part of the backpack kids (runners for the drug dealers), or you play ball. Well, my mother was so strict that not only did I play basketball, but I picked up baseball, football, and bowling (283-top score in bowling, not bragging). Sports

---

[7] Personal communication with the author.

became my safe place, and I wanted to learn all that I could about sports. As I look back over my life, sports NEVER let me down. Win, lose, or draw, sports protected me. Sports completed me. Sports literally saved my life.[8]

Jeff Trotter, Founder and CEO of Bend Dxnt Break

Thinking about sports makes me realize the major role that basketball played in my personal development as a man. Spending countless hours in the gym working on my craft kept me off the street and protected me from a life of crime, a life that led many of my friends to being incarcerated or to an early grave. I thank God for basketball because it was my outlet; it was my way out. It gave me the opportunity to travel the world and to be influenced by great men who never gave up on me. And just like they never gave up on me, I'll never give up on basketball. Regardless of how men and money make countless attempts to rob basketball of what it was designed to be at its purest, it will always be a great tool that intentionally develops athletes holistically to be their very best.[9]

Sports Credentials: All-Time leading scorer and rebounder at Creekside High School (GA); runner-up Mr. Georgia,

---

[8] Personal communication with the author.
[9] Personal communication with the author.

Robert Morris University. NBA G-League Canton Charge. International Travel Team Crossfire USA.

Eric Hasseltine, Play-by-Play Announcer (Memphis Grizzlies)

If we took the many lessons learned through sports to heart, it would make a huge difference in society. Meaning, it doesn't matter where you came from, what you look like, what your background is—economically, racially, religiously, or all of the above—when you're someone's teammate, you all work together for a common goal. You may not always agree with your teammates, but you always have their backs, and the goal is always the same. That goal is to be the best you can be, not only for yourself, but for your teammates.

Games are obviously about winning because we keep score, but in the end, you're not going to win every game. The lessons learned during a loss are sometimes more valuable than the joy of winning. Regardless of your level of play, as you play hard and work with your teammates, you learn important lessons about yourself and your interactions with others. And I believe that's the greatest thing about sports: you don't have to be great to get great things from the game.[10]

---

[10] Personal communication with the author.

Using Sports to Teach Life Principles

The sports scene has numerous testimonials like the ones above that function as exhibits in a museum. Each one is unique in its creation and priceless in its value. Sports have connected the dots for so many people though ironically, some people never realize it. Sports disregard factors such as gender, race, class, religion, and socioeconomic status to create unity. Sports bring millions of people together all over the world, causing them to play life's tunes through the song of sports.

The gospel song by William McDowell reminds us our life is not our own. When you think about it, many people in the sports community have this very song stuck in their heads, believing in their hearts that they owe their lives to sports. And rightfully so, because to a certain degree, sports have saved and rescued them.

Sports have been a lifeline and a breath of fresh air for so many people. But let's consider this: maybe, just maybe, God has used sports to preserve our lives and enable us to see sports in a different light. Maybe His game plan all along has been to share with us this great opportunity to appreciate the many life principles that are embedded within the game itself.

The idea of illustrating life principles through sports is not new. In fact, many coaches from the recreational end of sports to the professional end have taught life lessons through this vehicle called sport. However, *The Playbook* is unique in that it utilizes life-producing, killer crossovers that ankle break their way from sports to Scripture, revealing life principles' best shots. I fully believe that sports are a part of God's design for us to discover the practical principles hidden in His word, and maybe, just maybe, that's the reason we fell in love with sports in the first place. Maybe, we never chose sports, but sports chose us.

The GOAT Debate

Believe it or not, the "Greatest of All-Time" debate did not start with Lebron, Jordan, and Kobe. It started with Jesus's disciples in Luke 9:46–48 when an argument started among the disciples as to which of them was "the greatest." Jesus, knowing their thoughts, took a little child and had him stand beside Him. He said to them, *"Whoever welcomes this little child in my name welcomes me; and whoever welcomes me welcomes the one who sent me. For it is the one who is least among you all who is the greatest"* (Luke 9:48).

~You never have to try to be the GOAT; all you have to do is serve the Lamb.~

Welcome to *The Playbook*, where we use sports to unlock faith principles—principles designed to take us up!

PRESEASON

E arly in the spring of 2020, a pandemic shook the entire globe, including the sports world, causing all public events to come to a halt. Nonetheless, life continued, and the world kept spinning on its axis, forcing us to navigate through life without sports. But were we truly without sports, or were we simply able to navigate life during this crisis *because* of sports?

The Playbook gives us perspective as a sports community and shows that even pandemics are powerless to make the world of sports stand still! This is why we must never hopelessly wallow in our struggles because even when the game seems to be buried beneath the grave of unprecedented circumstances, sports rattle out with a defibrillated, resuscitated, and resurrected shout: "Open the grave; I'm coming out. . . . I'm gonna live again!"

For sports to gain supreme, lasting relevance, life can never just be about the game, but it has to be about the principles learned while navigating life's challenges. There is a game *beyond* the game that can only be discovered by treasuring the parallel, principled purpose buried beneath it. So, let's embark on an amazing journey together with the intensity of a "Warrior," the spirit of a "Sun," and the heart of a "King" to discover the "Nuggets" of wisdom and slivers of "Magic" that make the game that we cherish so dearly a true dynasty that transcends eras, never to be dethroned and lasting forever.

When I am with those who are weak, I share their weakness, for I want to bring the weak to Christ. Yes, I try to find common ground with everyone, doing everything I can to save some. I do everything to spread the Good News and share in its blessings. Don't you realize that in a race everyone runs, but only one person gets the prize? So, run to win! All athletes are disciplined in their training. They do it to win a prize that will fade away, but we do it for an eternal prize. So, I run with purpose in every step. I am not just shadow boxing. I discipline my body like an athlete, training it to do what it should. Otherwise, I fear that after preaching to others I myself might be disqualified.

—1 Corinthians 9:22–26 NLT

First Quarter:
EARNING YOUR STRIPES

Tigers and Lions and Bears, oh my! Hands down, one of the more popular mascots in all of college sports is the tiger! Why is that? Well, I believe that influence more than anything else has caused the popularity of the tiger as a mascot to grow across so many colleges and universities. We have the Auburn Tigers, the Clemson Tigers, the LSU Tigers, the Memphis Tigers (my favorite), and the list goes on and on.

Talking about the valued importance of influence is the perfect way to start this journey because sports have been a major influence in the lives of millions of people, even billions. As a matter of fact, I dare to say that sports carry a wave of influence that nearly everybody has surfed. Now here's the funny thing about it: many times you don't even realize that you are surfing on a sports-infused wave of influence until you are drenched by its ripple effect. Every wave has a beginning, starting its journey in the rough, tough trough and then crescendoing its way up to the pinnacled crest.

In looking at this great phenomenon, I can think of no better place to start our journey than in my own backyard, my hometown of Memphis, Tennessee. I grew up and fell in love with basketball and football on the neighborhood streets of Whitehaven, the southernmost part of Memphis. I'm talking about dirt courts, Make-It/Take-It, creating goals out of milk crates, playing games of 21, and challenging friends in the game of Elimination. I'm talking about sandlot football with house rules that changed every time you crossed neighborhood lines: 1-Mississippi, 2-Mississippi, rush the quarterback, pop on the sideline, two-hand touch in the streets, tackle in the grass, and "hot ball." I'm talking about drawing plays with sticks in the dirt. I'm talking about the good ole days, the glory days when your "Ma dear" would call out to you saying, "Boy, get yo' triflin' tail in this house! You know you're supposed to be in here before the streetlights come on, smelling like day-old sunshine."

The city of Memphis believed that the glory days had returned when a story roared down Beale Street, carrying the ponderous weight of a Tiger prior to the NCAA 2019–2020 basketball campaign. The University of Memphis Tigers basketball team, led by Coach Penny Hardaway, secured the #1 recruiting class in the entire nation. (Say what? Come again . . . Who?)

Yes, it's true. The University of Memphis beat out blue-blood schools like Kentucky, North Carolina, Duke, and Kansas to land the top recruiting class in the entire nation. Though this amazing feat is astonishing, the question of how it was accomplished can be answered with one simple word, *influence*.

Five-Star Recruit

When it comes to influence, the playing field is surprisingly level because *everybody* possesses the power of influence. So that begs the question of whether the influence we have on others will be positive or negative. Proverbs 27:17 advises, *"As iron sharpens iron, so a friend sharpens a friend"* (NLT). When people rub shoulders with us, we have a responsibility to make them better . . . to sharpen them and not to dull them out.

Full transparency: As I write this book, I am fighting against minimizing and discrediting my own power of influence and questioning the significance of my impact. I'm not a world-renowned author; there is no famed celebrity pedigree to my name, so why would anyone want to read something that I have written? Many times on this journey, I have had to tell myself, "Rickey, don't worry about what you don't know; just operate with what you *do* know." And what I do know is this: without a shadow of any doubt, God inspired me to write this book. So, I just have to believe that this book will carry the influence that it is designed to carry . . . period. So, I say to you, never ever underestimate your power of influence; instead, earn your Tiger stripes by placing a premium on how you influence others. We must do our very best to ensure that the ripple effects of our waves of influence are positive, remembering that all influence matters and is as priceless as a golden penny.

The Penny Effect

The *Cambridge Dictionary* defines *influence* as "the power to have an effect on people or things, or a person or thing that is able to do this." One of the most significant things that undoubtedly influences all people is relatability, which was one of the keys to Memphis securing the nation's best recruiting class of the 2019–2020 season. The recruiting class that Coach Penny signed for that season wanted to play basketball professionally. From D. J. Jeffries, who was once committed to Kentucky, to Boogie Ellis, who was once committed to Duke, all seven of the recruits aspired to play basketball in the NBA. Duke has multiple championships under Hall of Fame Coach Mike Krzyzewski and dozens of players who have successfully made it to the NBA. Kentucky has a super-rich history and was coached by John Calipari who has a resume full of first-round NBA draft picks. These factors may challenge your understanding of why a kid with aspirations of making it to the NBA would choose Memphis over such schools.

When you look at this conundrum through principle, you quickly discover that such recruiting results only happen when some level of trust is forged through relatability. And herein lies the answer to the mystery, which you will find is elementary, dear Watson: When a coach like Penny Hardaway looks like you, dresses with a swag that appeals to you (designer suits, Louis Vuitton belts, sneaker game on complete fleek), and has a swag that is arguably better than all the NBA superstars who you aspire to be . . . that's relatability. On top of that, Penny is the only NBA player not named Michael Jordan to have a signature basketball shoe that continued after his playing career. *That's* influence, an aspect of marketability that he can sell you on.

Coach Penny grew up in an urban neighborhood just like so many of the kids he recruited, and against the odds that came with this upbringing, not only did he make it to the NBA, but he played multiple years on a first-team, all-NBA level. When you have someone like him sitting in your living room, playing you in NBA 2K as himself, talking to you and your parents about your future in basketball, it's hard to say no. And parents who had witnessed his journey to the NBA and remembered the Lil' Penny doll and the *Blue Chips* movie would surely be impressed with his influence. When he tells you, "I played this game on a level that allowed me to overcome the very same odds you face, and I can help you reach your goals," it's hard to argue with that. Why? Relatability! Because he can relate to you, and his influence can make your dreams tangible.

A Penny's Value Is Greater Than One Cent
Penny believes he is doing what he was created to do according to God's plan; he believes that he was called to teach young men how to face adversity in ways that give them an easier path. Thus, he chooses to spend his time—the most valuable commodity that anyone has—dishing out assists to young men so that they are in position to make winning plays for a lifetime. Such a sense of purpose and commitment resonates within your heart and forges a relatability that is undeniable.

If the relatability of Penny's story doesn't register to the point of reliability, let's double down and add fuel to the fire in the person of Mike Miller. Coach Miller, Penny's first assistant and top recruiter during the 2019–2020 season is a guy none of the kids can outshoot; he is a former NBA Rookie of the Year, a previous NBA Sixth Man of the Year, and a guy who won two NBA championships with Lebron James. I know I had you convinced smack-dab between Lebron and James. With a guy like that working for Memphis alongside Penny, the kids aspiring to play college ball vehemently exclaim, "I don't care about your rich tradition, Kentucky. I don't care about your Hall of Fame coach, Duke. I want to be a part of this new thing happening at Memphis, playing for coaches who look like me, coaches who can relate to where I am coming from and who have been where I'm trying to go—coaches that I believe I can trust with my future. That's where I am influenced to go."

Blue-Chip Moment
We can only be the influence that others need us to be when we display a willingness to be vulnerably transparent. This gives people something they can truly relate to which makes all the difference in the world. Remember, as critical decisions are made, trust is always evaluated.

Oftentimes, as I evaluate what's most important to me, I can hear the Capital One commercial asking, "What's in your wallet?" What is most valuable to you? What is the currency pocketed in the wallet of your heart worthy of exchanging for? I'm reminded of a story in 1 Samuel 15:22 when Samuel learns that Saul, the king of Israel, had disobeyed God, and he says to Saul, *"Obedience is better than sacrifice"* (NLT). This statement compels us to look at our value system from the premise of comparison with the understanding that our value system influences our decisions. While rich tradition and legendary notoriety have their value, to these kids looking at playing ball for a college team, they pale in comparison to relatability because relatability trumps them both.

The Unicorn Effect

As we continue investigating how the University of Memphis landed the best recruiting class of the 2019–2020 season, we discover that the primary contributing factor was seven-foot-one, 240-pound James Wiseman. He was the McDonald's High School All-American, Gatorade National Player of the Year, Tennessee Class AAA Mr. Basketball, Morgan Wootten National Player of the Year, and 2019 #1 National Basketball Recruit.[11]

Wiseman was the consummate catalyst, the straw that stirred the Gatorade, the essential piece to Memphis securing the number one recruiting class. His commitment proved to be the ultimate bargaining chip that provided leverage for the Tigers signing stellar Top 50 athletes like Precious Achiuwa, Boogie Ellis, and Lester Quinones.[12] Wiseman's commitment was the "Absolute Power Move," the influential force that served as Memphis's weapon of mass construction. When they landed him as a recruit, a ripple effect that fully embodied the waves of influence was created. But what influenced Wiseman to choose Memphis over Kentucky, Duke, and the other blue bloods of college basketball? It's simple: history. Let's get our Digger Phelps on and do some more digging.

- **Exhibit A (Past Relationships):** Wiseman already had a relationship with Penny Hardaway, the coach at Memphis, and had developed a rapport with him.

---

[11] Wikipedia, "James Wiseman," last modified October 2, 2024, https://en.wikipedia.org/wiki/James_Wiseman.

[12] Evan Kurland, "Memphis Basketball: Scouting the Nation's No 1 Recruiting Class," May 21, 2019, https://fansided.com/2019/05/21/memphis-basketball-recruiting-class-analysis-expectations/.

He played for Coach Penny in high school and for his AAU team, which competed on a national level.[13]

- **Exhibit B (Previous Success):** As a junior, Wiseman won a state championship playing for Coach Penny at East High School (Tennessee), over my alma mater, Whitehaven High (Tennessee). As a sophomore, Wiseman only made it as far as the semifinals in the State Tourney while playing for Ensworth. And as a senior, still playing for East a year after Coach Penny left for the Memphis job, Wiseman successfully guided his team to the State Finals, but they lost to eventual champion, Bearden.[14] Clearly the pinnacle of Wiseman's success playing high school basketball happened while playing for Coach Penny, which had to be a factor in his decision to play for Coach Penny on the college level. He had faith that he would experience similar success and that his national ranking would be right where he wanted it to be—at the top.

Much in the Clutch

When you make guarantees and follow through on them, you establish relational capital. This capital earns you trust that goes a long way in building quality relationships and generating waves of influence.

Exhibit C (Precursory Bonds): Choosing to play for Memphis meant that Wiseman was going to play with friends

---

[13] Wikipedia, "James Wiseman."
[14] Wikipedia, "James Wiseman."

with whom he had already developed a brotherhood-like bond. He had played with Tigers' signee Malcolm Dandridge at East High and with the Team Penny/Bluff City AAU team for the previous two years. Wiseman and Dandridge were inseparable. Wiseman had also played with Tigers' signee D. J. Jeffries, who was also a member of the aforementioned AAU team. And Wiseman had won a state title with Tigers' PG Alex Lomax who was the assist man on many of his buckets at East.

What kid doesn't want to play basketball with their friends and for a coach they know they can trust? There is absolutely no way that these previous experiences did not influence Wiseman's decision to play for Memphis.

OK, let's do a really quick exercise, since we're in this together. Press Pause (don't worry, you're gonna press Play again soon) and take a quick perusal through your mental photo album of previous life experiences. I guarantee you will conclude that you have been heavily influenced to make decisions and be who you are today by your previous life experiences.

Half-Court Press

You must always guard your experiences with the dexterity of the 2019–2020 Tigers Defense (which led the nation in defensive field goal percentage) because previous experiences influence the decisions you make about your future.

Hall of Fame Speech

In the "living room where it happened," the confidence of NBA journeyman and Memphis Tiger great, Elliot "Socks" Perry, was instilled into the recruiting class of 2019–2020. This confidence led them to fully believe that when they came to play for Coach Penny, he would help them create a personal narrative that reads like his own, possibly even better:

- "Breaking news: The Memphis Tigers win their first ever national title . . . Rah!"
- "Extra, extra, read all about it: With the second pick of the 2020 NBA Draft, the Golden State Warriors select James Wiseman . . . Rah!"
- "News flash: With the twentieth pick of the 2020 NBA Draft, the Miami Heat select Precious Achiuwa from the University of Memphis . . . Rah!"

The "Memphinity Stones" is what I like to call the nation's #1 basketball recruiting class of 2019, mainly because they were convinced to play for the Thanos of college basketball recruiting, Penny Hardaway. Coach Penny convinced his 2019 recruiting class that by teaming up with the Memphinity Gauntlet, James Wisemen, they would be melded into an experience that would avenge their origin story, win them a national championship, and ultimately help them realize their NBA hoop dreams.

Quick Pivot and Drop Step

It is important to realize that the #1 recruit in the world, Christ Jesus, is that guy we should all be lining up to play with because playing with Him provides us with an advantageous leverage that enables us to cut down the nets of our purpose and our destiny.

Coaching Keys to Victory

As you carry out your plan of influence, remember:

- Your influence is always relevant, so never devalue it.
- Your influence is more efficient with a plan.
- Value substance over style by choosing effectiveness over aesthetics. Influence isn't always pretty.
- The same approach doesn't work for everybody. Realize when you need to switch it up for the sake of influence.
- Small ripples of impact create big waves of influence. Sometimes, what feels like a loss is really a win.
- You will take losses along the way; however, keep striving to be creative in your influence and do whatever it takes to maximize it.

"Earning your Tiger Stripes" starts with prioritizing your influence to the point that you see it as a rite of passage for living.

SECOND QUARTER:
MAMBA MENTALITY

It was Monday morning, January 27, 2020, and I was driving my son, Trey, to school. The drive that morning felt totally different from any other drive because I was driving in wake of the news that one of my sports heroes had tragically passed away. Laker legend and NBA great, Kobe Bryant, had been killed in a helicopter crash at the age of forty-one. I was forty-one years old. And to make matters worse, one of his four beautiful daughters, thirteen-year-old Gianna was also killed. My son was thirteen. This sorrowful misfortune was even more detrimental when we learned that other families were also killed in the crash. The sports community is my family. Selah.

We find the word *selah* often in a book of Psalms; it literally means to pause or to rest, to reflect. Before we read any further and speed past the sadness of this heartbreaking story, let's have a moment of Selah. Considering how fast life is and the fact that it stops for no one, we can easily find ourselves in a struggle to generate Selah moments—moments when we can pause and rest and reflect, moments when we can inhale and then slowly exhale, so let's do that now.

Take a deep breath in; then slowly breathe out . . . oh, trust me, you need it. Now reflect on your life and how blessed you are, how fortunate you are to be alive. Reflect on how blessed you are to be sitting on top of the ground, reading this book instead of lying beneath it—blessed to be looking at flowers instead of looking at roots.

Now pause and give thanks. You can take as long as you want. I promise you we will still be here when you get back. You aren't going to miss anything.

"Father, we thank you for life." Life is fast. I never say life is short because Psalm 91:16 says, *"With long life I* [God] *will satisfy him and show him my salvation."* But life definitely goes fast, so Father, we pause right now to appreciate the life You have given us.

At age forty-one, driving my thirteen-year-old son to school, I was in a state of disbelief and having a really tough time comprehending Kobe's unfortunate tragedy. I was struggling with understanding what afforded me the opportunity of driving my son to school the morning (mourning) after the world was devastated by the terrible news of Kobe Bryant's death. We're still here; it could've been us, but it wasn't. At the heart of my struggle was the question: "Why am I still here?" I know the ultimate answer is God's grace, but it still doesn't make sense.

Let me be the first to tell you that processing thoughts about God's grace is virtually impossible, so don't allow it to hang you up. The human brain isn't capable of fully comprehending the grace of God. But what we can do is apprehend the grace of

God by taking advantage of it. We fully take advantage of God's grace by (I must pause here to clear my throat and summon my Jill Scott voice) *living our life like we're Kobe, living our life like we're Kobe, living our life like we're Kobe . . . Kobe . . . Kobe.*

In no way, shape, form, or fashion am I insinuating that the way to take advantage of God's grace is by idolizing Kobe Bryant. So, allow me to explain my position by sharing with you my Lakers story.

My Lakers Story

I am what you would call a die-hard or as I prefer to say, live-easy Lakers fan. I like promoting life over death in keeping with Deuteronomy 30:19, which says, *"I have set before you life and death, . . . choose life"* (KJV).

I was born, raised, and currently live in Memphis, Tennessee, but I'm not a Memphis Grizzlies fan. Don't get me wrong, I root for the hometown squad, but I love the Los Angeles Lakers, primarily because my dad raised me this way.

I remember growing up and watching Lakers' games with him and hearing him talk to the TV saying things like, "Get Mychal Thompson [1978 top overall pick and Klay Thompson's dad] out of the game; he's sorry as buttermilk!" He would say, "Put Coop [Michael Cooper] in the game, Byron Scott's wet-behind-the-ears self can't make a wide-open shot!" He was passionate about those games, and it didn't take long for me to follow suit.

I grew up during the sports era when the Los Angeles Lakers ruled the basketball world. In the '80s, the basketball world was blessed with the opportunity of seeing NBA

Legend, six-foot-nine point guard Magic Johnson lead "The Laker Break." Fast-pacing, gracefully creating, dropping dimes to teammates like James Worthy, Byron Scott, and Michael Cooper for glamorous slam dunks. And when they slowed it down, Magic had the luxury of passing the ball down low to the second all-time scoring leader, Kareem Abdul-Jabbar, for his vintage, unstoppable skyhook. Man, those were the days . . . "Showtime Lakers," Baby!

As Kareem came to the end of his illustrious twenty-year Hall of Fame career, he was replaced by another future hall-of-famer and Serbian great, Vlade Divac. As great as Vlade was, his greatest contribution to the Lakers organization occurred on NBA draft night, the summer of 1996, when he was traded to the Charlotte Hornets for the rights to an incoming high schooler: the young phenom, Kobe Bean Bryant. Thank you, Vlade Divac, and Jerry West (former Lakers great and the general manager at the time) for making this happen.

But West wasn't through. That same summer, the Lakers acquired the services of Shaquille (Shaq) O'Neal, one of the most dominant centers of all time. Kobe went from being a high school senior like me graduating in the Spring of 1996 to making it to the NBA that summer, joining forces with Shaq, and forming what is arguably the greatest NBA one-two punch ever. This dynamic duo went on to win an amazing three NBA championships in a row (2000–2002)––in the most dominating fashion. I mean, they literally owned the NBA. And then the very world as they knew it, came crashing down as they feuded and eventually went their separate ways. Kobe remained a Laker, and Shaq was traded to the Miami Heat.

Of course, as it is with all fallouts, both sides contributed to their ultimate parting of ways. Both Kobe and Shaq were superstars, alpha dogs in the prime of their careers. Neither one was suited for playing second fiddle to anyone, which heavily contributed to the demise of their team's dominance.

Like Kobe

Kobe was extremely focused and determined to be the best NBA player of all-time. He even had the unmitigated gall to set his sights on being better than NBA great, Michael Jordan. He patterned his game after Jordan, and as his friend and former NBA legend, Tracy McGrady, said, "He damn near pulled it off."[15]

Recently, I was watching the "All the Smoke" television broadcast hosted by Matt Barnes and Stephen Jackson in which they interviewed Kobe. Kobe told them that he developed his first "kill list" (a list of basketball players to surpass in his journey to greatness) at the age of thirteen. At the time, he was ranked the 200th best basketball player in his class. He had cats like Tim Thomas, Mike Bibby, and Richard "RIP" Hamilton ranked ahead of him at the top. Naturally, they were on his "kill list."[16] Of course, by the time they were seniors, he had surpassed all of them and become the #1 high school basketball player in the class of 1996. He took this same drive to be better than all his contemporaries with him to the NBA and developed

---

[15] "Kobe Bryant," *All the Smoke,* created by Matt Barnes and Stephen Jackson, episode 11, Showtime, 2020.

[16] "Kobe Bryant," *All the Smoke.*

a determination not to let anyone outwork him.[17] This drive, this focus, this determination, this will, this edge created by a competitive nature that refused to be outdone by anyone on the planet became known as "Mamba Mentality."

As Kobe developed this mentality, he learned the importance of having a growth mindset versus having a fixed mindset. Now, in my estimation, mindsets fall into one of three levels: growth mindset, fixed mindset, or decline mindset:

- The decline mindset does just that; it causes one to essentially decline in their way of thinking. When operating with this mindset, a person allows experiences not only to challenge their self-esteem, but to lower it, causing them to think less of themselves. This is a mindset that we must absolutely reject by not allowing any situation to diminish our own view of self. Sometimes that can be tough, but we must refuse this mindset at all costs.

- The fixed mindset is an even more challenging one to fend off because most people who have this mindset don't even realize they have it. Have you ever thought or acted like you knew all there was to know about something to the point that you refused all other perspectives? If so, you were guilty of having a fixed mindset. This mindset is stealthy, stagnant, and stubborn. It has certain values and precepts that it holds true, to a fault, displaying an unwillingness to budge for anything or anybody. Because I grew up in a rich, conservative Baptist

---

[17] "Kobe Bryant," *All the Smoke.*

tradition, I developed certain views about religion as a young adult. During that time, those views were all that I knew. They were ingrained and deeply rooted in my mind. But one day, while sitting in a World Religion class at Strayer University, my perspective broadened. My professor started off the semester with a profound statement that I will never forget: "We all worship the God of our experience." One day in class, as my fellow classmates were sharing how their life experiences led them to believe in faith traditions that were different from mine, the scales fell off my eyes, and I realized that I had to give the same respect concerning their God that I wanted them to give my God. This moment flipped on a switch that allowed me to transition from having a fixed mindset into having a growth mindset.

The key factor that determines which level you fall into is what you allow to happen in your mindset as you go through life experiences. Are you stubborn to the point that you think one belief is the only correct solution, regardless of what happens, like a fixed mindset? Or do you allow life experiences to eat away at your mindset and cause you to either think less of yourself or diminish your perspective, like a decline mindset? The goal should be to have a growth mindset—a mindset that evolves when faced with an opportunity to conform. Our aim should be to develop a mindset that is stretched and strengthened with life experiences. If you peel back a few layers of Kobe Bryant's great basketball journey, you'll find this is the mindset that he developed over time.

Gigi's Sunlight

As you develop your mindset, value the importance of becoming a learn-it-all versus being a know-it-all.

Kobe's Remix Volume 2.4

A younger Kobe was fixed on being better than Michael Jordan, but the reason behind his fixation may surprise you. Believe it or not, Kobe, who grew up in the same era as I did, was a huge Magic Johnson fan. As a kid, one of his desires was to be six feet nine like Magic and to play just like him. In fact, growing up, Kobe's bedroom was enshrined to Magic Johnson.

So, where did this fascination with all things Michael Jordan—the way he walked, the way he talked, the way he looked—come from? Kobe's fascination with Michael Jordan peaked when he was identified by legendary Sonny Viccaro to become the pivotal charismatic piece to the evolution of the Adidas shoe brand.

In the mid '80s, Adidas flamed out on the opportunity to land Michael Jordan as the key cog to their shoe industry engine.[18] Later on, the impact of this mistake was realized as Jordan became a global icon, and Adidas, in an effort to regain relevance and compete with Nike, began searching for the next guy with the potential to have the same impact within the shoe market as Jordan did. They singled out Kobe Bryant, observing the similarities that he had with Jordan.

---

[18] Peter Verry, "Kobe Bryant Was 'The Second Coming of Michael Jordan,' Says Industry Veteran Sonny Vaccaro," January 27, 2020, https://footwearnews.com/2020/focus/athletic-outdoor/kobe-bryant-adidas-deal-sonny-vaccaro-michael-jordan-1202911153/amp/.

Jordan and Bryant were both six-foot-six basketball stars, played the same position, had a similar style of play, super athletic, and full of charisma. Each one's style of play had a unique personality and unusual flair that lit up every room that they stepped into. So, as Kobe hit the scene as a young phenom straight out of high school, he was singled out by Adidas.[19] In *Showboat: The Life of Kobe Bryant*, Roland Lazenby says:

> Even as a teen, Kobe was singled out by representatives of Adidas, the athletic-shoe company, and they told him that they planned to make him the next Michael Jordan. And because it was a role that lined up perfectly with his own goals anyway, within a few short months, he had the part literally mastered, from the speech patterns and mannerisms to the confident heir, even to the shaved head and Jordan-like charm.[20]

So, the answer to the question of whether Kobe Bryant was fixated on being Michael Jordan is 1,000 percent yes. But you can't judge him, because you would have been too. He was a kid straight out of high school, who already had the drive to be the best basketball player in the world. Give him a blueprint that he knows will help him to achieve that goal of greatness, and he'll be traveling and double dribbling down that path in a heartbeat.

---

[19] Verry, "Kobe Bryant Was 'The Second Coming of Michael Jordan'."
[20] Roland Lazenby, *Showboat: The Life of Kobe Bryant* (Little, Brown & Company), 2016.

The ultimate reason that Kobe Bryant is one of my sports heroes is not because he is a lifetime Laker with a great origin story, but because he changed numbers. Mid-career, after experiencing so much success wearing number 8, Kobe changed his jersey number to 24. This is significant because the change represented a switch that was flipped on inside his mind. As his jersey number changed, Kobe himself changed. He evolved from having a fixed mindset to having a growth mindset. He evolved not only as a basketball player, but as a person.

It's almost like he messed around and read Philippians 3:13, which says, *"forgetting what lies behind and reaching forward to what lies ahead, I press on toward the goal to win the* [heavenly] *prize"* (AMP). Kobe had a goal to win. But he realized that to do so, he had to shift his mindset because the mindset that gained him success in his past would not garner the same success in his future.

Change can be a hard pill to swallow especially when it comes to changing your way of thinking. It's hard realizing that the things that led to your previous success will become null and void in your future success. For this reason, one of the biggest enemies of future success is previous success. Here's what Kobe said about changing jersey numbers:

> When I first came in as 8, it was really like this trying to "plant your flag" sort of thing. I got to prove that I belong here in this league. I've got to prove that I'm one of the best in this league. You're going after them. It's nonstop energy and aggressiveness and stuff . . . Then 24 is a growth

from that. Physical attributes aren't there the way they used to be, but the maturity level is greater. Marriage, kids. Start having a broader perspective being one of the older guys on the team now, as opposed to, being the youngest.[21]

Kobe evolved, just like we have to. Kobe learned that he didn't need to have a kill list to become great. The more mature version of himself learned that being obsessed with mastering Michael Jordan would never help him accomplish his ultimate goal. He learned that obstacles can either become stumbling blocks or steppingstones. It all depends on perspective. He learned that there was no need for him to compete for a share of the limelight with Shaquille O'Neal or anybody else for that matter. All he had to do was focus on being the best version of himself. The only person that he needed to compete with, the only person that he needed to chase, was his next best version.

If you think that I am still talking about Kobe Bryant, then you're missing it. No, I'm talking about *you*. The only person that you ever need to chase is your next best version.

As you transition from better to best, you must understand that you can never become the *best* version of yourself without first becoming a *better* version of yourself. Choose progress over perfection. That's exactly what Kobe did. He kept getting better;

---

[21] Nicco Martinez, "The Real Reason Why Kobe Bryant Changed His Jersey from No. 8 to No. 24," Fadeaway World, last updated August 8, 2022, https://fadeawayworld. net/.amp/nba-media/the-real-reason-why-kobe-bryant-changed-his-jersey-from-no-8-to-no-24.

he kept growing. He kept working on his game, transforming weaknesses into strengths to become arguably one of the best NBA players of all time.

- Mamba Mentality: A drive that refuses to lose, a will that leaves nothing in the tank, a seam-bursting determination that penetrates every ceiling that lies above it.
- Mamba Mentality: an undeniable force that overcomes every obstacle that stands in front of it, an intense focus that works when rest is desired, an infectious energy that drives the very best out of everyone that it touches, a mindset that exhibits an uncompromising willingness to evolve.

If we are to live out our full potential and become the best version of ourselves, we have to live our lives like we're Kobe by developing a Mamba Mentality.

Mamba Out

There are so many popular sayings that highlight the importance of one's mentality: "The mind is a terrible thing to waste," "An idle mind is the devil's workshop," "My attitude determines my altitude," and so on. A perpetual tug of war is going on inside us, and our minds are always the victor's prize. Picture a wrestling match, of sorts, in which your flesh and spirit are in a battle royale for your mind, trying to control the way you think, trying to influence what you meditate on. If we are going to be the best versions of ourselves, our spirit must consistently break the will of our flesh and seize control of our mind.

Coaching Keys to Victory

As you develop a growth mindset, remember:

- You already know what you know, so prioritize learning what you *don't* know.
- When you ask questions before making statements, the impression you make is that you value understanding over being understood. The general practice of understanding encompasses all, while being understood focuses more on you.
- Having a valid argument doesn't always validate arguing. A wise person first counts the cost. You never want to win meaningless debates and lose meaningful relationships.
- Whatever dominates your thinking will dominate your actions and ultimately dominate you. Think about what you think about and meditate on what you meditate on!

Don't copy the behavior and customs of this world, but let God transform you into a new person by changing the way you think. Then you will learn to know God's will for you, which is good and pleasing and perfect.

—Romans 12:2 NLT

Halftime:
TRUST THE PROCESS

The Israelites, God's chosen people, were promised a land flowing with milk and honey, yet they wandered in the wilderness for forty long years before ever getting to claim it. This happened to illustrate the truth that valuing process is critical to promises being fulfilled. Many prominent basketball players utter similar words into microphones when faced with challenging situations that they must overcome to achieve success. They say, "I worked for this moment. And I just have to trust the work that I put in. You know, just trust the process." As you prepare for life's challenges, remember that "preparation time is never wasted time."

Patient Offense

Though the Israelites were given the "Promised Land," they were assigned to the wilderness for forty years, which means they were forced to wait. Our wilderness seasons are grand opportunities to learn the process of waiting for God. When we don't learn how to wait for God, our seasons of wilderness are prolonged. We must realize that waiting for God's promises to be fulfilled is not a dormant activity. We must not "waste time" during our "wait time." The Israelites struggled learning this lesson, which led to them being in the wilderness for a long time.

> *For in this hope we were saved. But hope that is seen is no hope at all. Who hopes for what they already have? But if we hope for what we do not yet have, we wait for it patiently.*
>
> —Romans 8:24–25

In 2021, before my daughter, Ryane, arrived in this world, my wife, son, and I were waiting expectantly for her. God promised this miracle to our family and though His promise had been conceived, we still had to wait for Him to deliver it. What my family had to do was make ready for the fulfillment of this promise. We had to prepare and practice so that we would be in a position to receive God's promise. You don't wait for the baby to come and then buy diapers and prepare the nursery. You prepare the home for the baby before the baby comes home. You see, we could not be dormant in our waiting, but we had to proactively wait for God to fulfill His promise. This is what "process" is all about.

The Origin Story

In 2013, the Philadelphia 76ers started rebuilding their franchise on a foundation called "Trust the Process." In many cases, sacrifice is found at the genesis of process, which holds true in this story. The chief decision that launched this movement was made when general manager Sam Hinkie sacrificed the 76ers' best player, All-Star Jrue Holiday, for Nerlens Noel, an injured draft pick who had torn his ACL during his lone season at Kentucky. When criticized about this major head-scratching move, Hinkie's response was, "We're rebuilding, and fans just have to 'trust the process!'"[22]

> *Trust in the LORD with **all** your heart and lean not into your own understanding; in **all** your ways submit to him, and he will make your paths straight.*
> —Proverbs 3:5–6 emphasis added

This is one of the most powerful proverbs of all time. It is exceptionally profound at its core, but it is also extremely challenging as it is manufactured out. The preponderance of its challenge is unveiled with two words emphasized conjointly: *trust* and *all*.

I have found that trust, which means to firmly believe in something or someone, is the ultimate process in and of itself. It seems like as soon as you believe that you've mastered trust in your heart, a voice rings out from the rubble of circumstance that sounds just like the father who exclaimed in Mark 9:24, *"I do believe; help me overcome my unbelief!"* Have you ever been in a situation that made you realize that your belief system wasn't as firm as you thought it was? That's because trust is a continual

---

[22] Max Rappaport, "The Definitive History of 'Trust the Process'," August 23, 2017, https://bleacherreport.com/articles/2729018-the-definitive-history-of-trust-the-process.

process—because life is a series of episodes that ends in the cyclical cliffhanger: "to be continued."

And just in case the perpetual procedural operation of trust isn't enough by itself, the word *all* is thrown into the mix, like a second-round draft pick in a bad trade. The small three-letter word *all* thrusts trust into a place where it becomes the alpha dog of process. There is no way around it. Trusting with all your heart has to be processed all the way out.

It's easy to trust with just a portion of your heart because you're not fully invested; therefore, you have nothing to lose. When you're not fully invested, every prospective blow of disappointment is cushioned or suppressed, so even when you're called out, you're still safe. It's like having an unlimited cell phone plan or unlimited lives in a video game. The risks are minimal at best. But when you start talking about trusting someone or something with all your heart, the stakes are much higher. There is no gray area, no living on both sides of the fence. No, you're all in, my friend, and trusting on a level of this magnitude simply requires process.

The Process of Surrender

During the "Trust the Process" era of the Philadelphia 76ers, they made another major move by hiring Coach Brett Brown in 2013. Brown, who had gained a championship pedigree with the San Antonio Spurs winning four NBA titles as their top assistant, was identified as the franchise's choice to lead the new regime.

In Brown's first year coaching the 76ers, they went 19–63 and lost a record-setting 26 games in a row. His second year was consistent with the first as they recorded a win-loss record of 18–

64. But it is this next part that is mind-blowing. After starting his third season with eighteen straight losses, you would have expected Brown to be fired. But in the franchise's worst season ever, a season in which they finished 10–72, the Philadelphia 76ers extended Brown's contract.[23] This seemed to be utterly bananas when you consider the rate at which they were losing; nevertheless, they gave him an extension. This grandiose gesture proved that the 76ers fully believed that Brown was the right guy to lead them into a successful future as they trusted the process.

Contract Extension

Trusting God requires us to become fully invested in a way that compels the organization of our hearts to extend His contract, indubitably making Him our coach, even in our franchise's worst season. I acknowledge the challenge associated with this level of trust, especially when you consider that everybody wants to win now. We live in a success-driven, triumph-salivating culture that tries to make everything transactional. We're essentially saying, "Before I give you anything, first let me find out what I am getting back in return." When we constantly seek the hand of God and not the face of God, that affects our ability to trust Him with all our heart. The Bible says:

> *This Book of the Law shall not depart from your mouth, but you shall meditate in it day and night, that you may observe to do according to all that is written in it.*

---

[23] Scott Polacek, "Brett Brown Signs 2-Year Contract Extension with Philadelphia 76ers," accessed November 2, 2024, https://bleacherreport.com/articles/2596754-brett-brown-contract-latest-news-and-rumors-on-negotiations-with-76ers.

*For then you will make your way prosperous, and then
you will have good success.*

—Joshua 1:8 NKJV

As we unpack this verse, we quickly notice how its step-by-step process determines good success. First, it references monitoring what comes out of your mouth, then it talks about habitually meditating on what you meditate on. Last, it lists measuring how you observe. Like an old Baptist preacher closing out a sermon, this single verse highlights these three points as being strategic for us arriving at the squalling, whooping, grand finale of good success.

Here's the kicker: if there is a thing called good success, there must be a thing called bad success. Bad success is any type of success you achieve outside the will of God—success that does not honor His process.

Allow me a moment to tell you a brief personal story free of judgment. At present, I am happily married to the woman of my dreams, an absolute godsend whom I love dearly. Before my current marriage, I was married to my first wife, my son's mom; that marriage ended in divorce. Well, in between these two marriages, I was engaged to yet another woman; that was single-handedly the biggest mistake that I have ever made in life.

I was never truly in love with her; however, I was head-over-heels in love with the conventional idea of marriage and family. These ideals were stripped away from me first in my youth when my parents' marriage didn't work out and then again when my first marriage failed. So, I attempted to reach my desired result of establishing marriage and family without honoring the process.

That was a grave mistake. Thankfully, I called the wedding off and dodged that bullet, and the rest is history. Considering what could have been and what presently is, I am compelled to give God my biggest extension of praise: "Thank you, Jesus, for my now-and-forever wife and my family!"

Signing Bonus
The moment you start prioritizing results over valuing process is the moment you start trampling on your path to good success and short-circuiting your ability to trust God with all your heart.

Crossroads
Again, the foundational passage of Scripture reads, *"Trust in the Lord with all your heart, and lean not into your own understanding; in all your ways acknowledge Him, and He will direct your paths"* (NKJV). Notice that in this passage, there is a proverbial fork in the road that forces us to choose a path.

Traveling down one path calls us to trust God with all our heart; traveling down a different path calls us to lean into our own understanding. There is always a crossroad when we encounter situations in life where we have to make tough decisions. Will we trust God with all our heart, or will we lean into our own understanding?

Let's take away any mystery that may exist about the word *understanding.* Your understanding is what you stand under, like an imaginary overhead purification system that goes wherever you go. All your ideas are processed through your understanding. It is your understanding that provides your emotions with a protective perspective when storms arise. Your understanding is the governing body for all your thoughts—the authoritative presence that influences all your expectations.

Let's swiftly throw the vehicle of our comprehension in reverse and drive back to this crossroads. When we consider the magnitude that one's understanding carries, it would appear that the logical path for us to go down is the one of least resistance—that is, leaning into our own understanding. Naturally, this is the logical choice to make, but sometimes situations become illogical. They don't add up, and they don't make sense. Situations arise that simply don't fit into our system of deductive reasoning. Those moments challenge us to go beyond the rationalization of our natural perspective and force us to *"trust in the Lord with all our heart."*

Eye of the Storm

Trusting God with all our heart intrudes on our natural human perspectives by helping us to see challenging situations as opportunities to worship Him. Trusting in God also enables us to view depressing conditions designed to oppress us as opportunities for fellowship with Him. Yes, irrational storms that transcend cyclical weather patterns will rage in your life, tempting you to question God's power and authority. My encouragement is that you surrender to God in these moments instead of yielding to the winds and the waves of the storm. These storms are but menial opportunities for God to give us a testimony in our test, a message in our mess, and a chance of a lifetime to bless others.

Trusting God When You Can't Trace Him

My son, Trey, absolutely loves to draw. In fact, he's pretty good at it. Sometimes, he will stay in his room for hours at a time drawing and doodling; he even studies videos on how to draw certain characters. His ability to draw is a talent that I first noticed when he drew characters from the animated movie *Zootopia*. The picture that he drew was so impressive that I asked him if he traced it! He assured me that he did not trace it, which later observation proved to be true, but he admitted that sometimes he does trace.

When Trey traces pictures, he pulls the image up on his phone, places the phone beneath his drawing paper, then traces the image, which nine times out of ten is a Marvel character. Every time he traces an image versus drawing freehand, he does so because he doesn't believe he can attain a desired result without tracing, or he just wants to take a shortcut to reach that desired result. The other thing that I realized with tracing versus freehand drawing is that I don't appreciate the drawing as much when he traces it, because *anybody* can trace, which means there is no true separation of gift and talent.

It's much easier to trust God when you can trace Him, when all your expectations are met, when the circumstances of life don't seem to be getting the best of you, or when all is well. But can you trust Him when you can't track or trace his presence? Will you choose the right path when you bring out the German shepherd K-9 squad and the scent that they pick up leads down the path of your own understanding without acknowledging God?

As for the path of trusting God with all your heart, there are no tracks, no scent to be followed, no trace of God's presence. It seems at times that there are no desired results and no met expectations. In that case, will you still trust the process? Will you still seek God's face when you can't see His hand? Or must His hand at least be in your peripheral view for you to seek His face?

At the height of seeking God's hand are our expectations of Him, and when those expectations are not met in a specific time frame, it challenges our ability to seek His face. It challenges our ability to honor the process of totally trusting Him with all our heart.

God desires us to trust Him enough to give Him a freehanded extension, one in which we worship Him and greatly appreciate Him for who He is and not for what He has done. He desires that we yield to Him all our gifts and talents, so that He can use them for His glory.

The Process of Healing

The next step in the Philadelphia 76ers' process was to start building up through the NBA draft, and that's exactly what they did. With the third pick in 2014, they drafted the seven-foot Cameroonian center from the Kansas Jayhawks, Joel Embiid. In his lone season with the Jayhawks, Embiid missed both the Big 12 tournament and the NCAA tournament due to a lingering back injury sustained in Big 12 play. As he began his NBA career, injuries followed him. A nagging foot injury caused him to miss his first two seasons entirely.

After healing from multiple surgeries and dealing with several setbacks, Embiid made his long-awaited debut in what was his rookie campaign during the 2016–2017 season.[24] He played extremely well as a rookie, but would find himself sidelined

---

[24] Michael Shapiro, "From Embiid to Simmons to Smith, Is There an Injury Curse with 76ers' Rookies?" August 8, 2018, https://www.si.com/nba/2018/08/08//6ers-rookies-injuries-curse-joel-embiid-ben-simmons-zhaire-smith.

by injuries once again, missing the second half of that season. Can you imagine the anxiety that must have overwhelmed Sixer Nation as they waited for Embiid to heal? I'm sure they wondered whether he would ever play again. Was he a bust? Did the organization do its homework before acquiring what appeared to be damaged goods? Of course, general management was aware of the many questions and concerns fans posed, but to their credit, they refused to allow these rumblings and grumblings to rush the much-needed process of healing.

An extended healing process was also needed for Ben Simmons, drafted by the Sixers with the number one overall pick of the 2016 NBA draft. After a successful 2016 NBA Summer League, Simmons sustained a foot injury during training camp, which sabotaged his entire 2016–2017 season.[25] No. Not again! Not another foot issue! Not another entire season lost. I'm sure many Sixers fans exclaimed, "We can't win for losing." But, since we're speaking of winning, Simmons would return during the 2017–2018 season, which was his official rookie season, and win Rookie of the Year.

During that season, the Sixers finally got what they had been long awaiting. Simmons and Embiid were on the floor at the same time, foot injuries a thing of the past. This talented and healthy duo ultimately led them to some success and the playoffs for the first time since 2012.[26]

In both injury-ridden situations, the setbacks were pinned to the notion of not healing properly. In different seasons of

---

[25] Shapiro, "From Embiid to Simmons to Smith."
[26] Shapiro, "From Embiid to Simmons to Smith."

life, we find ourselves drafting individuals in search of finding winning combinations to help us excel. Unfortunately, injuries beyond our control are sustained along the way, introducing the importance of healing properly to win. Setbacks are never fun, and, with violent disregard, they disrupt our timetables, causing us to feel like we are going backward instead of forward. Nevertheless, a premium must be placed on healing the right way. Grieving, lamenting, isolating, fasting, praying, abstaining, and navigating seasons of loneliness can all be stages in a proper healing process. These distinctive and distinguished steps prove to be pivotal parts of a process that primes, prunes, and positions us for continued success.

Truth be told, the Sixers organization could have had a pity party as the pivotal cogs in their engine of success sustained injury after injury. They could have felt sorry for themselves as it appeared their "process" came fully loaded with damaged parts and injured accessories. As soon as they drove their luxurious "process" off the lot with drive-out tags still bringing up the rear, the engine light came on with no way to turn it off. As they ran diagnostic test after diagnostic test, they could have attempted to fill voids not unlike construction workers pouring gravel into the sinking potholes of Memphis streets to prevent the derailment of their trajected path to success, but they did not. That would have been like putting a Band-Aid on a broken arm.

Don't get it twisted . . . the Sixers organization was totally engrossed with the idea of building an NBA championship contender through their "process" much like I was utterly mesmerized by the idea of building a family through marriage. Thankfully, unlike me, they did not allow a ticking timetable to speed up their "process" like I did with the in-between fiancé. They wisely responded to their inside and outside noise by allowing their injuries to heal from the inside-out.

Physical Therapy
It seems as though life comes prepackaged with expectations that are graphed like ticking time bombs on a timeline, which cause us to be date-driven and not data-driven. A huge proponent of "process" requires us to accumulate data and then respond based on that data. You will find that sometimes before you can progress through process, you have to properly heal from the wounds created by unmet or mismanaged expectations.

The Process of Forgiveness

The Sixers organization also identified opportunities where they simply needed to "cut their losses" and move on from the Sixers' Ghosts of Draft Picks Past (previously drafted acquisitions that didn't pan out the way they envisioned). In 2017, they traded Nerlens Noel, the player whose procurement began their whole "Trust the Process" narrative. In that same season, they traded Jahlil Okafor, the player who was drafted with the third pick in the 2015 draft after he won an NCAA championship in his lone season at Duke. Though the highly acclaimed center showed signs of being a solid contributor early on, the logjam presented at center when Embiid returned proved to be too much. So, after only two and a half seasons with the organization, the Sixers moved on from Okafor.

Something else remarkable happened during the 2017 season. The Sixers had the number one pick of the draft yet again. What great luck! They used that pick to draft Markelle Fultz from the University of Washington, but the former #1 overall pick did not even complete two full seasons with the Sixers before they traded him away. Sound familiar? Rightfully so, because during the 2014–2015 season, they traded Michael Carter-Williams not even a full year after he won Rookie of the Year.

These moves prove that the Sixers general management were not afraid to "cut bait" with what could be identified as poor choices or unprofitable decisions in the grand scheme of what they desired to accomplish. They vehemently refused to allow the mistakes of their past to haunt them, but instead forgave themselves and moved on. Forgiveness will always be one of the most critical components in our ability to heal.

All-Time Great

Here is something to consider as we process forgiveness. At the foot of the cross, a silent, bloody Jesus on the precipice of crucifixion was being beaten, when He mutters these words recorded in Luke 23:34: *"Father, forgive them, for they don't know what they are doing"* (NLT)! Yes, Jesus forgave the people for doing what they did to Him while they were still in the process of doing it to Him. Amazing! The forgiveness that was displayed in that moment can only be depicted as "premeditated forgiveness," an immediate forgiveness that is extended before the offense ever takes place.

Yeah, I know what you're thinking: "But it's Jesus," right? It's because He was Jesus that He was able to pull off this fairytale-like degree of forgiveness that's beyond our human comprehension. But the problem with thinking like this is that you fail to consider the hypostatic union, in that Jesus was 100 percent God and 100 percent man. So, the 100 percent man side of Jesus, the side with which all humans can identify, struggled with forgiveness just like we do. However, He persevered in a way that allowed Him to forgive immediately.

If we're honest, this is just not how forgiveness typically works for us. First and foremost, before we even consider forgiveness, the action that is being forgiven must no longer be active. Second, but equally important to us, is that we need time––however long we say it takes––to heal from the offense against us before we even consider forgiveness. Last, many of us would also appreciate an apology before we extend forgiveness.

But Jesus shows us another way. And it's not because He is 100 percent God or 100 percent man, but it is because He is 1,000 percent purpose. Jesus doesn't consider his hypostatic union as He is forgiving the world from a place of pain. That fancy terminology is for us. Philippians 2:5–8 proves this by saying:

> *In your relationships with one another, have the same mindset as Christ Jesus: Who, being in very nature God, did not consider equality with God something to be used to his own advantage; rather, he made himself nothing by taking the very nature of a servant, being made in human likeness. And being found in appearance as a man, he humbled himself by becoming obedient to death—even death on a cross!*

Jesus was so focused on His assignment that He didn't even consider the hypostatic union as He carried it out. He was so heaven-bent on His purpose that He refused to allow anything like unforgiveness to block His path. In fact, He had forgiveness already prepared for our future offenses. While we were yet sinners, Jesus died for us. It's like forgiveness was Jesus's dying wish for us. Not "like,". . . that's *exactly* what it was! When you realize that your purpose is great, you simply don't have time to harbor negatives like unforgiveness. "Premeditated forgiveness" speeds up our healing process and allows us to continue down the path to the great purpose assigned to us. The real question that you must ask yourself when you are struggling to forgive is this: "How great is my purpose?"

The Process of Humility

Another phenomenal thing happens in Philippians 2: we are shown what optimized humility looks like. Verse 8 tells us that Jesus humbled himself in obedience to death. It's a pretty major deal to be immortal, then willingly become mortal, only to schedule your death. Ultimately, that's what humility is all about—a willingness to die to yourself.

The Sixers organization was humbled as they faced the tough reality that there were deficiencies within the infrastructure of their "process" that could not be resolved through the NBA draft. If they were ever to build a team that would compete for multiple championships, they needed veteran leadership, and they needed to address their weakness of perimeter scoring by converting it into a strength.

Instant Classic

Acknowledging that you are deficient in areas of your life and addressing them in such a way that you convert them into strengths is the checkmate of all things humility.

In a process of humility, the 76ers began addressing the weaknesses of both their roster and philosophy by signing sharp-shooter JJ Redick during the 2017 off-season. Then they traded for Jimmy Butler and Tobias Harris during the 2018–2019 season. These humble moves landed the Sixers in the Eastern Conference Semifinals where they lost in Game 7 on a buzzer-beater to the eventual NBA champions, the Toronto Raptors. And though their "process" continued, principle had arrived.

The one definite thing that optimizing humility calls for is consistent and transparent honesty with yourself. For me, this translates to acknowledging my persistent battle with hypersensitivity. I am forever thankful for the reminders found in Scriptures such as 1 Peter 5:5–6 in which Peter says, *"God resists the proud, but gives grace to the humble. Therefore humble yourselves under the mighty hand of God, that He may exalt you at due time"* (NKJV). At its core, being hypersensitive is a result of pride and thinking too highly of yourself. Ouch!

The issue of my hypersensitivity is something that I have been dealing with for a while; however, I just finally realized it. Super early on in my relationship with my wife, even before we were officially a couple, I realized that I was way too sensitive. On our very first date, she said some things to me that legitimately hurt my feelings and knocked me off my high horse. And, let me tell you, "Mighty was the fall, because all the king's horses and all the king's men couldn't put me back together again." But the King could!

I could have very easily given up and crawled back into my hole and stopped pursuing her altogether. But she was different in the way that she challenged my intellect and my perspective, so I couldn't give up. In that moment, as I found myself stuck between a rock and a God place, I was forced to ask myself a tough, hypothetical question: "Rickey, if a person is getting on your last nerve, is the issue what they are doing to get on your last nerve or the fact that your last nerve is exposed for them to get on?"

The answer to this question allowed me to look at the emotional makeup of my sensitivity and helped push me forward. So, I kept pursuing her and confronted the things she said to me, not with my own words, but with the Word of God. Jackpot! This got her attention, causing her to ask her friends, "Who does he think he is to challenge me with the Word of God?"

Now we were at an impasse where she had piqued my interest by challenging me intellectually, and I have piqued her interests by challenging her spiritually, leaving us both intrigued enough to keep going. As time progressed and we got married, I became cognizant of the fact that my wife represented more than something I wanted, but something that God wanted to give me.

My self-talk went something like this: "OK, God, let me get this right! Evidently, you have created this woman for me, and she is passionately strong-willed, outspoken, and displays confident, intellectual intelligence that has the potential to constantly challenge my sensitivity level in the most intimidating fashion. God, you can't be for real."

As my interest in her grew and things became more serious, it became more apparent that I had to actively address my hypersensitivity, or else I would become an emotional wreck. So, I began to categorically identify my level of sensitivity as a weakness and started addressing it by seeking to understand how I had become so sensitive in the first place. It turns out that the root of my sensitivity stemmed from rejection during my adolescent years, which intensified later in life when I felt abandoned by people that I thought had accepted me.

This core trigger of heightened sensitivity led me to this place where I continually sought approval and affirmation from others. As a matter of fact, "words of affirmation" is my primary love language. If I wanted to keep things progressively moving forward with my wife, I had no choice but to get my hypersensitivity in check.

Ultimately, I decided to embrace all of her—the good, the bad, the ugly, the indifferent. And in embracing all of her, I released some of myself—most notably my pride—which allowed me to love the parts of her that were initially challenging for me to love.

Is it possible that God is trying to give you something, but you're too sensitive to handle it, so you miss out on it completely? Is it possible that a lack of resilience causes you to abandon meaningful relationships instead of living in the necessary tension of a moment? Is it conceivable that because you're wearing your emotions on your sleeves, you lose focus on the position of your hands?

This is a prime opportunity for consecration because consecration literally means to release what is currently in your hands so that God can fill your hands with what He wants you to have. Is it possible that we are missing out on what God has for us because our hands are full of things that God never intended for us to have? This is a question that you must answer for yourself. And in answering it, you may find that this is the appropriate time to enter into a season of consecration.

Practice, Not the Game, But Practice

Our level of sensitivity can cause us to raise defenses unnecessarily, which stunts the growth of our perspective, which is the way we view ourselves and the way we view others. Our purview of life needs to grow for us to maximize our influence; being hypersensitive is counter-productive for that growth.

There have been moments in my life when I have allowed the mismanagement of sensitivity to cause relatively minor situations to blow up like overinflated basketballs. As I humbly acknowledged this as a deficiency, I gained enough courage to finally ask for help. By the grace of God, I received help by acquiring the person of the Holy Spirit, which added sensibility to my sensitivity. He continually helps me to remove the hyper from my sensitivity with the understanding that it is not a one-time fix, but more of a case-by-case situation.

In most situations, I have learned to become hypersensitive to my hypersensitivity through humility aided by the Holy Spirit, which empowers me to balance my reactions. We must always practice refining what has already been defined, so that we can become redefined.

Coaching Keys to Victory

As you trust the process, remember:

- You need the insured protection of process; though it may not be popular, it is always necessary. Essential things such as character, resilience, and determination are all built through process.

- The beauty of process is realized as the burden of process is removed.
- Fall in love with consistently working diligently. Embrace, endure, and enjoy the process of hard work, realizing that the promises and principles of process never shift.
- Allow the destiny that awaits you on the other side of process to provide you with the power to pull through.

THIRD QUARTER:
FORTY MINUTES OF HELL

I was talking to a friend one day who was having some Baby Mama Drama, exclaiming that, "She was the Donald Trump of baby mamas because of how erratic she was!" As he expressed his frustration to me, a light bulb turned on. He realized that the contention between the two of them stemmed from their competition to be the better parent. The fact that she was obsessed with proving she was a better parent than him caused them to constantly be at odds as co-parents, which negatively affected the child. And herein lies the danger of comparison traps.

The purpose of their relationship was to jointly parent their child, but that got lost in the mix because of comparison. Comparison traps present themselves like piranhas, constantly and aggressively trying to eat you up every second you are in their presence.

Comparison traps remind me of the relentless and suffocating defense played by the '90s Arkansas Razorbacks basketball team, which was coached by Nolan Richardson.[27] That shriek you just heard was from the opposing SEC teams who are still having nightmares about the defensive pressure of Richardson's Razorbacks.

The Razorbacks played a style of defense that constantly put pressure on the other team—over the entire 94 x 50 feet of the basketball court, for the entire forty minutes of the game. This style of play came to be called "40 Minutes of Hell," where the Razorbacks' top priority was to force their opponent to succumb to their pressure. They wanted to make the other team try to be something that they were never designed to be.

Their in-your-face, harassing defense never allowed opponents to feel comfortable, which consequently caused them to make mistake after mistake, creating turnover after turnover. Coach Richardson realized that he needed a deep bench to pull off this style of defensive basketball. And that's exactly what he had, but not a bunch of blue-chip guys, otherwise known as players who would go on to have stellar NBA careers. In fact, Corliss Williamson, aka "Big Nasty," was the only player on Richardson's most successful squad to get drafted as a first-round pick in the NBA.

Instead, his team was stocked with blue-collar guys who fully bought into his defensive style of playing basketball. These

---

[27] "SEC Storied: 40 Minutes of Hell," July 11, 2020, https://www.secsports.com/article/11113347/40-minutes-hell.

were guys who flourished in a system that rewarded them for playing hard-nosed, physically intense defense. This style led to their winning a national championship in 1994.[28]

I was blessed to talk with fellow Memphian, Dwight "Big Sy" Stewart, a champion from that squad who recalls what it was like to play for Coach Richardson. He said, "Coach would tell us if we don't score, they don't score! He didn't care if we missed shots, as long as we defended." Stewart, who played center for the Hogs at six feet nine and 265 pounds, recalled Coach Richardson telling him, "I know you play center, but I don't care if you have to check a guard all game. If you want to touch the floor, you better be able to do it. Move your feet!" And guess what Stewart did . . . he moved his feet.

Stewart said they were young and hungry, and Richardson made them believe they could do anything. That's why they were able to play defense the way they did. The mastery of this intense style of aggressive defense is akin to the traps we fall into every time we believe the deceitful and societal noise of comparison.

Transition Bucket

The world has created a distracted culture that fully measures success based on surface-level accomplishments in comparison to our peers. This diseased ethos harasses us out of character and speeds us up, making us play faster than we should. Consequently, it places us in situations that don't allow us to fully take

---

[28] Nate P., "Nolan Richardson Talks About the Origin of That '40 Minutes of Hell' Label," March 11, 2011, https://www.swishappeal.com/2011/3/11/2044606/nolan-richardson-40-minutes-of-hell-arkansas-razorbacks.

advantage of our strengths. In addition, this culture causes us to miss out on opportunities to celebrate the accomplishments of others, all in the name of hating by comparison. This distracted, diseased culture causes us to experience way too many turnovers concerning our ball, which is purpose. As we know, you simply can't win without the ball. Ultimately, comparison traps can give us either:

- A sense of superiority, making us feel better than the person with whom we are comparing ourselves, which leads to pride.
- A sense of inferiority, making us feel worse than the person with whom we are comparing ourselves, which leads to low self-esteem.

The solution to this toxic cycle of opposites, which are in some ways, one and the same comes from the same verse:

> *Make a careful exploration, evaluation, or examination of who you are and the work you have been given, and then sink yourself into that. Don't be impressed with yourself. Don't compare yourself with others. Each of you must take responsibility for doing the creative best you can with your own life.*
> —Galatians 6:4–5 MSG

It is not coincidental that the antidotal principle that pulls us out of the pit of comparison traps is from the same verse because, regardless of what end of the spectrum we are on, the way out is the same.

Full Court Trap

When we succumb to comparison traps, we neglect and abandon our very own unique assignments. These assignments are designed to help us take advantage of our strengths while empowering us to strengthen others. They intrinsically close the deficit of the ever-present weaknesses in humanity. We can ill afford to leave these assignments incomplete due to being comparatively trapped outside of grace.

Attempting shots outside your hot zone of character causes shooting percentages to decrease, which directly results in an extremely low player efficiency rating. So, the quick halftime adjustment that we must consistently make is to avoid comparison traps at all costs if we are to maintain our player efficiency.

OK, Razorback fans, I see your champions: Corey Beck, Dwight Stewart, Scotty Thurman, and Corliss Williamson, and I raise you champions from the Bible: Daniel, Shadrach, Meshach, and Abednego—comparison trap conquerors.

In Daniel, chapter one, the Lord allowed His people (Judah) to be exiled to Babylon because of their previous disobedience to His will. Nebuchadnezzar, king of Babylon, surrounded Judah and sieged it, forcing the Israelites into captivity. Then, King Nebuchadnezzar ordered for some of the Israelites from Judah's royal family to be brought into his service. He wanted handsome young men without any physical defect who showed aptitude for every kind of learning. He required that they be well-informed, quick to understand, and qualified to serve in the king's palace.

Nebuchadnezzar wanted to teach them the language and literature of the Babylonians. He wanted to assign them a daily amount of food and wine from his table and train them for three years, after which they were to enter the king's service. Among those chosen from the royal family were Daniel, Shadrach, Meshach, and Abednego.

Daniel, along with his friends, declined the king's offer of choice foods and wine and asked the chief official for permission to eat vegetables and drink water instead (which were part of the diet the Lord had commanded). The chief official, whose assignment was to build up the strength of those in training, responded with, *"I am afraid of my lord the king, who has assigned your food and drink. Why should he see you looking worse than the other young men your age? The king would then have my head because of you"* (Daniel 1:10). Daniel bargained with the steward, who was left with the responsibility of administering the royal delicacies, and said to him:

> *Please test your servants for ten days: Give us nothing but vegetables to eat and water to drink. Then compare our appearance with that of the young men who eat the royal food, and treat your servants in accordance with what you see.*
>
> —Daniel 1:12–13

Convinced, the steward agreed, and at the end of the ten days, Daniel and his friends looked healthier and better nourished than any of the young men who had eaten the royal food. So, Daniel and his friends were allowed to eat and drink according to their regimen.

Avoiding Coffin Corners

When we constantly surrender to a corrupt system that only focuses on surface-level accomplishments instead of focusing on our God-given purpose, it may very well appear that we are in training although we are actually in captivity. Comparison traps can be tricky like that, persuading and convincing us that we are operating within our purpose when we are actually being held hostage outside God's grace. That is why we have to avoid these traps and never allow them to get us cornered.

One method of avoiding these traps is to become innately aware of implicit comparison traps or traps that we fall into by comparing ourselves to others unconsciously. The key to evading such traps is to steer clear of knee-jerk reactions, where your action is simply a reaction to others, not an action inspired by your purpose.

The story about Daniel and his friends, which I have labeled "No Cheat Meals," is so powerful in that it highlights the importance of keeping your established regimen with God, even when the world pressures you to do something different. Daniel and his friends simply refused to take the world's advice (more like a command), and instead they challenged it with God's truth. They contested the world's evaluation of an individual matter by putting it through trial-by-fire, which allowed them to see the world for what it was—calling a spade a spade and putting a name with a face. In removing the makeup from the face of the world, James 4:4 says, *"You're cheating on God. If all you want is your own way, flirting with the world every chance you get, you end up enemies of God and his way"* (MSG).

The world will lie to you repeatedly, fabricating narrative after narrative. It'll say to you, "This is what success looks like," or "you're not successful unless you're doing X, Y, Z, and the third." We have to develop the defensive prowess of the '90s Arkansas Razorbacks when it comes to exposing the lies of the world with the light of truth.

Help-Defense

The Word's illuminating offense by design shows us where the world's help-defense is coming from and positions us to tell the world to "Get the 'L' out of here!"

Ain't nobody got time to take an L (Loss). By allowing this great illumination to eliminate our Ls, our "40 Minutes of Hell" is converted into "40 Minutes of HE" with an understanding that when we constantly devote time to the Word of God, we are provided with strength from "HE" to help us overcome the defense of the world for the entire game of life.

For as much as God wants us to walk in the light of truth, the world is equally determined to point out all the things that we desire in life but have not yet acquired. The world forever highlights the things that it has decided we need, creating within us a sense of entitlement. And if that's not enough, the world puts a spotlight on the people who have acquired these things, which leads us down a discontented road of trouble. Sounds a lot like the world of Facebook and Instagram, doesn't it?

In the interest of not offending anyone, let me talk about myself for a second. Many times, as I get my "Social Media Scroll" on, I easily include myself in this world that I speak of. Though oftentimes I want to blame Satan or "the world" or anybody but me for the traps I fall into, I have found that my worst enemy is the (in-a-me): my very own self. Most every time, as lies are introduced and fallacies are presented, they have a little truth mixed in, which makes them harder to recognize and more difficult to refute. The only way to become fully cognizant of these untruths and canards is by saturating ourselves with the truth itself: the Word of God. If we know the principles from Scripture, we can sort the lies out from the truth. John 8:32 says, *"The truth shall make you free"* (KJV).

Focus on the Lord and the precious gift of His Word and Spirit when you are tempted to compare yourself with others. King David, whom God called a man after his own heart, was given armor to wear when he was about to fight the massive giant, Goliath. The armor was too large for his small frame. But instead of going to search for different armor so that he could replicate others who went out in battle, David focused on God's character and not his opponent. David focused on God's track record with him, and he knew that the same God who helped him and his people so many times in the past would continue to help him as he faced Goliath. I believe that if we pause to think, we can all recall experiences when God has come through for us. This is important because to become the champions that God has called us to be by design, we must constantly remind ourselves of His faithfulness.

Most Outstanding Player Highlight Moment

We simply cannot afford to fall into the debt of comparison because the expensive price that we pay plunges us into the "Base Salary" category. This is the category that is established every time we base our ceiling on what the next person is making instead of transforming our ceilings into new floors to turn a profit. Remember, the best version of yourself is always processed through your better self and never based on others.

My paraphrase of Colossians 3:23–24 would read like this: "Whatever you do, do your very best, as though you were doing it to please the Lord and not to please people. For there is no comparison when it comes to how people reward you versus how the Lord rewards you. Work for the Lord and not for people. Serve the Lord, Christ."

Stretch Four

Our relationship with Christ stretches far beyond a mere association with Jesus because it represents the mantle, the authority, the position, and the anointing that He operated within to fulfill His purpose. The very same anointing is available for us to operate within, and the quicker we focus on capturing this anointing (versus being comparatively captivated by the world), the sooner we can fulfill our purpose through Christ.

Coaching Keys to Victory

As you avoid comparison traps, remember:

- One of the keys to realizing who you are is to realize who you are not.
- Even as you learn from a mentor, be careful not to allow lines to be blurred that cause you to lose sight of your identity.
- Being a carbon copy of someone else depreciates the originality of your potential. A good version of you will always be better than your best version of someone else.

Fourth Quarter:
BULLSEYE PERSPECTIVE

If I were the two-time NFL Champion, Michael Strahan, hosting the sports edition of the game show "Pyramid" and I gave you the category "Bullseye Perspective," what would that category be about? That's right, the Chicago Bulls. But not the Bulls led by Jerry Sloan or Artis Gilmore or Derrick Rose.

The year was 1996, better known as the year that Michael Jordan and the Chicago Bulls won the franchise's fourth championship in the most dominating fashion ever. I mean, they were *crazy* dominant that year as they set an NBA regular season record of 72–10, eclipsing the 69–13 mark set by the 1972 Los Angeles Lakers led by Jerry West and Wilt Chamberlain.

As I reflect on 1996 Bulls, I remember it being Michael Jordan's first full season back in the NBA after a brief retirement stint, during which he flirted with baseball. Quick timeline update: Jordan led the Chicago Bulls to three consecutive NBA titles from 1991 to 1993, then he retired to play baseball, only to return during the NBA 1995 postseason playoffs. During

71

these playoffs, his Chicago Bulls lost to the eventual Eastern Conference Champs, the Orlando Magic, who were led by Penny Hardaway and Shaquille O'Neal. Jordan would lead his team to avenge this loss in the 1996 NBA playoffs, as they would sweep this same Magic team on their way to debatably the greatest season in NBA history.

It's super easy for me to remember the dominance of Michael Jordan and Scottie Pippen during this unbelievable run, as they are by far the best combination of two-way wing teammates to ever play in the NBA. Any comparison is not even close. This mega-talented super-duo would go on to win a total of six NBA championships in the fashion of two separate three-peats. Several unsung heroes in this dual-phased dynasty are not nearly talked about enough.

First and foremost, the hero that many people don't seem to remember is their defensive supremacy. The Bulls' defense simply reigned superior during their championship runs, especially in the second phase of the three-peats. I remember my dad saying to me as a young whippersnapper, still wet behind the ears, "The thing that sets the Bulls apart is not Jordan or their offensive efficiency. It's that other teams simply can't score on them in the fourth quarter. They shut them down. As I watched *The Last Dance*, a 10-part documentary series that covered the Bulls' final championship year, my only wish was that it focused more on their Doberman-like defensive superiority.

In my defense, there were years in their second stint as three-peat champs when they either led the league or ranked in the top four of every defensive statistical category, including opponents' field goal percentage, three-point field goal percentage, assists, and their overall defensive ratings.[29] Can I tighten the clamps of this point further? The numbers in these statistical categories got increasingly better in the fourth quarter of games and as they entered the playoffs. As I analyze this, I realize that in order for a team to arrive at this level of defensive dominance, they must have a gladiator, an enforcer, if you will. On the Bulls' teams of the late '80s, that person was Charles Oakley.

Oakley was a great rebounder, a solid defender, and a deadeye shooter from midrange. He was like the team's bodyguard— the guy that *nobody* wanted to cross. After "Oak" was traded to the Knicks for Bill Cartwright, the Bulls needed a new guy to fill the role of "enforcer." This new guy came in the form of Horace Grant, who was already on their roster having been drafted the year before. Grant was a key cog in the engine of the first Bulls three-peat championship run. He is a four-time NBA All-Defensive player, the team's third leading scorer, and their leading rebounder.[30]

After Grant left for the Orlando Magic, the Bulls' enforcer spot was left vacant for a year, later to be filled by Dennis Rodman, who wormed his way into this position. Dennis "Worm" Rodman was the ultimate enforcer. Originally, a Detroit Piston bad boy, he was a former two-time NBA defensive player-of-the-year, seven-time reigning rebounding leader, and an eight-time NBA all-defensive player. There is absolutely no way that you achieve a degree of mastery that

---

[29] "Basketball Reference-Chicago Bulls," https://www.basketball-reference.com/teams/CHI/.
[30] "Chicago Bulls History," Sports Mockery, https://www.sportsmockery.com/chicago-bulls-history/.

leads to all those incredible accomplishments unless you fully know, understand, and relish your role.

Rodman, who was an integral component of the Bulls' second round of three-peats, would spend countless hours watching film, studying his opponents and their tendencies, and identifying their weaknesses so that he could dominate them defensively. Despite all the personality concerns of who Rodman was off the court, he fully knew who he was on the court.

He was the proletarian, "wear your hard hat" and "bring your lunch pail to work," blue-collar worker who incessantly designated himself to do the dirtiest of the dirty work. This multi-color haired, heavily tattooed, globally pierced Hall of Famer who was viewed as a misfit, never cared about scoring a bucket and never had plays run for him. All he cared about was playing defense, getting rebounds, and nagging the crap out of his opponent. He fully embraced his role. It's almost unheard of for a player to play in a total of seven games during which he grabs at least twenty rebounds and scores zero points.[31]

Rodman, the energetic engine of the Bulls' defense, used spirited and passionate rebounding to provide extra possessions for his team while taking away possessions from their opponents. And, friends, having more possessions than your opponents will always be an ingredient in your recipe for success. Rodman didn't have to score buckets to make an impact; he knew exactly what his assignment was. And his ability to carry out that assignment made him one of the unsung heroes of the Bulls' championship success.

---

[31] Wikipedia, "Dennis Rodman," last modified October 3, 2024, https://en.wikipedia. org/wiki/Dennis_Rodman.

Instant Replay

Consider this lineup. You have six-foot-six two-way swingman Michael Jordan (Defensive Player of the Year, three-time Steals leader, multiple-time All-NBA defender) defending one position. You have six-foot-eight NBA First Team defensive do-it-all superfreak and NBA steals leader wingman Scottie Pippen, who could guard all five positions. You have six-foot-six Ron Harper, who ranks top 25 all-time in steals, defending yet another position. Rounding out this group of defensive-mastermind juggernauts is six-foot-seven Dennis Rodman, whose defensive and rebounding ability (13.1 rpg) landed him in the Hall of Fame, defending another position. With these four at the helm, roaming the court like Dobermans, the fifth person on the court, basically just had to be tall, and he surely was. Insert seven-foot-two center, Luc Longley, and initiate "Operation Lockdown!"

Private Workout Session – The Beauty of Rebounding

Rebound: to regain possession of the basketball after a missed shot attempt. Many of us can still hear our coaches shouting, "Hustle to the ball. . . . Get the rebound!" The reason behind this warranted energy is that coaches realize you simply can't win without the ball. Every single time you hear the word *rebound*, you should realize the value of possessing the basketball. Typically, the team that leads in this statistical category (rebounding) wins the game. And herein lies the power of the prefix *re-* because it represents the power of the "do-over" and empowers us to try again. With the prefix *re-*, you find words that we simply cannot

75

live without, like *refresh, renew, revive, reflect,* and *remember.* The prefix "re" re-presents the power of a second chance, and even the power of grace. We all *need* grace because without it, life, love, and faith would all be impossible.

To secure this concept with some consistency, there has to be a clear understanding that misses will occur, so never allow them to catch you by surprise. The reality is that we will miss certain shots in life, so the most rational thing to do is to anticipate missed shots. As you go through life, know that people will offend and hurt you. Having a mentality that prioritizes rebounding snags those moments of hurt by anticipating the offense so that you can quickly recover.

Anticipating missed shots quickens your response time. Have you ever missed a shot and immediately knew why you missed it? Naturally, all you want is a do-over, a second chance. Rebounding presents you with that opportunity—an opportunity to say to yourself, "I want that look again because I know what I did wrong, and I am confident that if I get another shot, I am going to make it." Rebounds provide you with that shot. They provide you with multiple opportunities to make an impact.

Most of our targets have potential as big as Goliath, but unfortunately, our shooting percentages are not as high as David's was, and we need more than one shot to hit our mark. So, we have to get our Charles Barkley on and become "The Round Mound of Rebound" to ground our gigantic destiny.

When a person anticipates missed shots, they can fight early to properly position themselves to secure rebounds. Effective rebounders understand that proper positioning is a critical component of rebounding efficiently. Have you ever heard the saying, "That person just has a nose for the basketball"? Well, nobody really has a nose for the basketball, but players who become great rebounders study and prepare to understand the different shot angles and how they factor into the way the ball caroms off the rim. It is important that we become familiar enough with our shot that we can anticipate our misses and position ourselves to regain possession after every miss.

Box-Out

When you realize that you absolutely cannot win without the ball, you will feel a desperate urge to always get the ball back. Rebounding is essential to winning in life, and losing is simply not an option.

Zen and Yang

Proverbs 4:7 says, *"Getting wisdom is the wisest thing you can do! And whatever else you do, develop good judgment"* (NLT). The wisest thing that the Chicago Bulls did aside from drafting Michael Jordan was hiring Coach Phil Jackson. Jackson's impact on the Bulls' success is remarkable, as he proved to be a well of wisdom that never ran dry. The way he managed his teams' personalities was nothing short of ingenious, as he knew all the right buttons to push to get the very best out of each player.

As Jackson coached, he modeled a statue of wisdom that was versatilely shaped by Asian philosophy. This philosophy provided him with a universal, holistic approach toward coaching[32] that whistled its way into the heart of Bulls' culture.

---

[32] *The Last Dance Limited Documentary Series,* directed by Jason Hehir (2020, ESPN Films and Netflix).

As we develop our perspectives and purviews of life, we must allow wisdom to be our coach, heeding her advice even when we don't feel like hearing it. I'm sure there were plenty of times when the Bulls' players were anxious to get some shots up or rush into the more practical components of their game plan, but I can imagine Phil Jackson, aka "The Zen Master," saying, "Before we work on these free throws and triangle, let's free our minds in this Yoga Circle!" Wisdom offers a perspective-shaping, life-changing, game-time decision that is critical for continued success.

We find that verse after verse in Proverbs encourages us to go after wisdom, referring to her as a woman worthy of the chase. Wisdom slows everything down and helps us to process everything; she is analytical in her ability to understand the perspective of others, even when they don't agree with her perspective. Like food, she fills our perspective with both substance and sustenance in a way that helps us avoid simplicity and folly. Adaptability and flexibility are two adorning jewels of wisdom's crowned glory as she honors those striving for prudence with her royal presence.

Put Me in the Game, Coach

We have to stop benching wisdom and giving her DNPs, for she is the star player that leads us to victory. She shouts out instructions such as, *"Iron sharpens iron; so a man sharpens a friend's character"* (Proverbs 27:17 ISV) and *"Better is open rebuke than hidden love. Wounds from a friend can be trusted, but an enemy multiplies kisses"* (Proverbs 27:5–6).

Jackson illustrated wisdom that transformed the Bulls from an organization into a family, from a team into a brotherhood.

Did they always see eye-to-eye? Of course not, but as the adage says, "Teeth and tongue may fall out, but they still stay in the same mouth." As you establish your bullseye perspective, remember, "A friend loves at all times, and a brother is born for a time of adversity" (Proverbs 17:17).

Think FAST

As we pinpoint the attributes that make up our team, we must think FAST—faithful, available, skillful, and teachable.

As the Bulls' unsung hero story continued to unfold, we noticed that their roster was filled with players who fully embraced their roles. This included faithful players such as Ron Harper who displayed a willingness to make sacrifices for the overall betterment of the team.

In the fall of 1994, the Chicago Bulls acquired Harper after he had been a superstar for the Cleveland Cavaliers and the LA Clippers (I still don't fully understand how Cleveland could trade Harper and their draft picks to the Clippers for Danny Ferry and Reggie Williams, but anyway). At the time of the trade, Harper was averaging 22 points, 7 rebounds, 7 assists, and 2 steals. As a matter of fact, Harper's first eight seasons in the league proved that he was a consummate scorer. He averaged nearly twenty-three points per game as a rookie and was still averaging twenty points a game in year eight, the year before coming to the Bulls.[33] But here is the proverbial kicker: the Bulls didn't need him to be their primary scorer.

---

[33] Colton Jones, "No one from Cavs wanted to trade Ron Harper . . . except the man whose opinion mattered most," last updated May 18, 2020, https://www.si.com/nba/cavaliers/nba/cavaliers/nba-amico/ron-harper-trade-cavs-bulls.

And to make matters worse, they didn't need him to be their secondary scorer, either. Instead, they needed him to help the team create turnovers by defending perimeter players with his length and become their secondary ball handler, setting up their offensive sets.[34]

Harper's extreme sacrifice on the offensive end and total buy-in on the defensive end was very impressive and ultimately made him a champion. Regarding his sacrifice, Harper said:

> I didn't complain last year. . . . I just knew I had to learn a lot. I know I've grown since last season [the '94–'95 season when the Bulls benched him as he struggled to embrace his new role]. My attitude has changed. I know some players in this league probably couldn't change the way they used to do things [transitioning from being a primary scorer]. I just wanted to be part of a championship team.[35]

Michael Jordan observed:

> [Harper] could have easily fallen off and gotten mad because he hadn't really been given a fair shot, but he stepped it up and said, 'Hey, I'm going to contribute in whatever fashion.' Most guys who have averaged 25 points and been the star on another team, it's hard for them to take a back-seat

---

[34] "Harper Shines Brighter in Light of Defense," *Chicago Tribune*, updated August 19, 2021, https://www.chicagotribune.com/news/ct-xpm-1996-06-18-9606180013-story.html.
[35] "Harper Shines Brighter in Light of Defense."

role in another system and find a niche where they can fit in and be successful. Not Ron . . . I'm really happy for him.[36]

Harper's ability to change his attitude and shift his mindset from being a player-first offensive force to a team-first defensive powerhouse was critical to the Bulls' success.

A very popular quote that has been used by Hall of Fame coaches like Bill Parcells and Bill Belichick is this: "Your most important ability is availability!" Or, as my friend Hatchett says, "If you stay ready, you don't have to get ready. . . . I always keep one in the chamber." Hatchett is an officer of the law who excels at basketball, so go figure.

The Bulls' rosters were filled with knock-down shooters like B. J. Armstrong, John Paxson, and Steve Kerr who stayed readily available to make open shots whenever their number was called. As a sort of luxury item, the Bulls had the tremendously skillful Croatian sensation, Toni Kukoc, who was the unsung hero that never stopped singing. This NBA Sixth Man-of-the-Year Award winner was consistently the Bulls third leading scorer and was literally a matchup nightmare. He stood six feet eleven and had the ability to shoot the deep ball, create his own shot off the dribble, and make plays for teammates. You couldn't guard him with a small forward because he would shoot right over them, and you couldn't guard him with a power forward because he would drive right past them. He was like Dirk Nowitzki before we knew about Dirk Nowitzki—at

---

[36] "Harper Shines Brighter in Light of Defense."

least in relation to being a matchup nightmare—because Dirk wasn't really trying to drive the ball past anyone.

All these players, whether they fell on the hero end of the spectrum or the unsung hero end of it, were teachable. They mastered the triangle offense taught to them by legendary coach, Tex Winter, in a way that allowed them to understand every intricacy of its design.

Understanding roles and relishing assignments definitely served as critical pieces to the Bulls' puzzle of championship success, and that's what having a bullseye perspective is all about. It's all about playing your position and staying ready for the moment with an unwavering belief that you are a critical piece of the puzzle. Thematically speaking, having a bullseye perspective is all about, "Knowing your role and shutting your mouth." Since I'm from Memphis, a place where Jerry Lawler is "The King" of wrestling, let me say it like this: Having a bullseye perspective is all about humbly submitting to your assignments, but knowing when it's time to "Pull the Strap Down" and get more aggressive within your assigned role.

Forming a bullseye perspective can easily start with one question: What can I do to make the greatest impact given my current situation? This is the question that Ron Harper had to humbly ask himself. The answer (Allen Iverson) to this question when responded to with the truth (Paul Pierce) gives our perspective an intense focus that allows us to acquire a target and aim directly for its bullseye. It enables us to identify that sweet spot as we take our shot at life and empowers us to sing the words of the hit musical *Hamilton*: "I'm not throwing away my shot!"

Hot Zone

A huge component of successfully living life is assiduously staying on mission to figure out that sweet spot within your purposed perspective.

Here's a quick story to illustrate the point. There was once a young, aspiring archer who visited a small town. Upon aimlessly journeying through this town, he found himself in a mystical forest where he was surrounded by dozens of trees. To his surprise, every tree had a bullseye drawn on it. The direct center of these targets had been pierced with perfect shots, and above each bullseye was an inscription that said: "Buzz did this!" (Buzzwords . . . get it?)

So, the aspiring archer said to himself, "I've got to find out who this Buzz guy is. A master archer, responsible for countless perfect shots. . . . I just *have* to meet him." So, he started asking around town trying to figure out a way to meet Buzz. He later discovered that, in town, Buzz was not known as a master archer; instead, he was known as the town fool. It turns out Buzz would shoot his arrow at the tree, making his mark, and then he would draw the bullseye around it.

The moral of the story is that only fools take shots where there is no target in sight and later define that mark as perfection. We must always know what we are aiming at by fully understanding our assignments and humbly embracing our purpose. Establishing goals, setting markers, and creating momentum are all critical to acquiring a bullseye perspective. If we look at the anatomy of the word *Bullseye*, we will find that a "bull" is symbolic for strength, determination, and confidence. Spiritually, the term *bull* represents being firmly rooted in Christ and having a good, solid work ethic.

The term *eye* is best represented by the term *perspective*, as the two terms can be used interchangeably. These terms symbolize an increased sense of perception and awareness and are commonly associated with qualities such as intelligence and moral conscience. The Bible discusses "perspective" in Proverbs 29:18 (based on multiple translations), and can be expressed this way: Where there is no vision [no redemptive revelation of God, who He is and what He is doing], then the people perish [they lose restraint, run wild, and become ungovernable].

God's First Choice

As I sought to gain a bullseye perspective, I realized that God took the perfect shot when He chose you. You are God's Plan A—His first choice. You're not some glorified afterthought; you're not God's last resort, and you're not some last-ditch effort. God wasn't desperate or out of options when He chose you.

With one shot, God set His eyes on you, and He hit the bullseye! You represent God's best shot—His only shot at accomplishing His purpose through you. That's why you are here. That's why you exist. You're God's first choice. There is no Plan B, and though I'm not trying to put pressure on you, I am trying to make you aware of this fact: Only you can accomplish the purpose God placed inside you. It's yours to achieve, so if you don't get it done, it won't happen.

For instance, God gave me this book that I am writing. He gave me the revelations. He gave me the words. He gave me the analogies. He gave me the illustrations. Everything that He has given me is unique to my experiences, my personality, and to my relationship with Him. No one else exists in the entire world who can present these revelations, these analogous illustrations, or this principled perspective in written form the way that I am because it is unique to my purpose in Christ.

You have a unique purpose that only you can accomplish, and when you realize the importance of this truth––the fact that you are God's first choice and there's no backup plan––then you will ultimately make God your first choice and place Christ at the center of your perspective.

Secret Place

God chose us so that we can lock our focus on the bullseye and choose Him. The bullseye, the spot, the point, the period in the center of the target not only represents God hitting the bullseye when He chose us, but it represents the place of pivot, which lies deep within the pinnacle of our perspective.

This pivot represents a place of change—a place where the bullseye is turned inside-out, designed to draw out everything that God has placed inside us. For Christ Himself constructed this meeting place. He tore the veil that separated us from God, resurrecting this sacred space, the Holy of Holies, the innermost part of the temple, for us to spend intimate time with God our Father. We can openly and freely express desperation for His will in this place. This is a place where I don't just seek the hand of God, but a place where I seek His face.

What I love most about this place is . . . Shhh! It's a secret. I don't have to tell anybody about it; I don't have to explain to anybody where I am, and I don't have to get permission to go. I can just go. Thank God that appointments are not necessary, and walk-ins are accepted.

As I walk into this sacred space, I sense that no matter how long I've been away, His presence is always there to encounter me. He's been waiting for me . . . waiting for me to express a desire to deepen my relationship with Him, waiting for me to familiarize myself with His voice. So, I can stop guessing what He sounds like and begin to *know* what He sounds like.

Oh, there is a place, a secret place, a place where I can go . . . a place where I can sit with God, a place where I can dine with God, a place where I can worship Him in spirit and in truth, so that answers are revealed, healing flows, and deliverance comes. It is a place where I can experience the fullness of His joy—a meeting place where I can cry out to God from the depths of my soul and get caught up in His presence.

Target Practice

So, we have our perspective: the science of optics, the lens that contains our purview of life, the way in which we perceive ourselves and others. Within our perspective falls our sphere of influence. Within our sphere of influence falls our scope of responsibility. Within our scope of responsibility should be consistent actions that lead people to Christ.

Within the scope of *my* responsibility, I take a stance that says, "Everyone who steps foot into my sphere of influence will realize that Christ is at the center of my perspective." Therefore, the way I perceive myself is filtered through Christ; the way I view others is filtered through Christ, and my outlook on life is filtered through Christ. He is my primary focus, and everything else is secondary.

Catch this: when you have to fight for your perspective every day (and you do), it is important to establish Christ as the intrinsic center of your perspective and to make everything else revolve around Him. Christ is not Jesus's last name; the word *Christ* comes from the word *Christos*, which literally means, "the anointed one and his anointing."

Christ is the mantle in which Jesus operated, and because of His sacrifice, He made this anointing available for us to also operate within. Therefore, our aim, our goal, our target, our bullseye is to operate within the same anointing in which Jesus the Christ operated as we take our shot at life. Christ **is** the bullseye.

Coaching Keys to Victory

As you understand perspective, remember:

- Invest in social circles that challenge your perspective. A challenged perspective is a conducive perspective.
- The foundation of perspective is life experience. To properly value the perspective of others, you must be able to see life through their eyes.
- In every situation, there is a different perspective that matters just as much as yours. So, rather than assigning too much weight to your perspective, soberly remember that opinions are not facts, and that perspective is not truth.
- Respecting the perspective of others is one of the keys to discovering the truth, which is the primary goal of perspective.

Late Game Heroics

Respecting the perspective of others does not necessarily mean accepting or embracing their perspective. In fact, it could very well mean respectfully rejecting it. Matthew 16 tells us that right after Jesus enshrines Peter into the Hall of Fame for declaring that He was the Messiah, He had to reprimand him. In Matthew 16:15, Jesus posed a question to the disciples asking, *"Who do you say I am?"*

Peter answered, *"You are the Messiah, the Son of the living God"* (Matthew 16:16). Jesus affirms Peter's perspective on who He is as truth and credited God as the source. Immediately thereafter, Jesus gave the disciples more truth by telling them that He would have to die, but that He would be raised from the dead three days later.

Though Peter realized the first truth, he struggled with accepting the second. This is mainly because his level of discomfort regarding the second truth caused him to examine the source improperly and to act out of his emotions. So, an emotional Peter pulls Jesus, the source of all truth, to the side and "corrects" Him. Jesus's response to Peter's version of reproach was of classic proportion and overflowing with respect.

Jesus turned and said to Peter, *"Get behind me Satan, you are a stumbling block to me"* (Matthew 16:23) because Peter was only seeing things from a human perspective, not from God's perspective. Jesus rejected Peter's perspective by quickly identifying and addressing its source and staying focused on His destiny. As a matter of fact, He didn't even bother with directly addressing Peter because it was never personal. Jesus's response had nothing to do with His relationship with Peter and everything to do with His relationship with destiny. Some perspectives will make you feel uncomfortable; they will be expressed in ways that cause you to become emotional. You can respectfully manage these perspectives by examining their source before addressing the personality behind them. Remember that every perspective has an origin story that must be acknowledged with respect to foster truth.

Overtime:
MEET THE REAL MVP

A wise man once said, "Perspective is powerful in that it undergirds understanding and influences interpretation." That wise man is me, but I digress. Understanding and interpretation are two major factors of life that are as huge as seven-foot-six NBA great, Yao Ming, which further highlights the importance of perspective.

Different people can read the same information and gain a level of understanding that renders dissimilar interpretations. This phenomenon holds true with how the Bible is interpreted and understood. One person could read the Bible from a Jewish perspective, while another could read it from a Christian perspective, and yet another could read it from an Islamic perspective. One book viewed from three different perspectives can lead to three different interpretations.

Just in case you didn't know, there is an infuriating war going on. A battle has ensued, weapons have been deployed, and the stakes are very high. The thing that is at stake is your perspective—your most valuable possession—your MVP. In this war, we fight for our perspective every day. We constantly face both people and situations that are trying to gain critical control of our MVP. You must be cognizant of the fact that your perspective is unique to who God created you to be. That is why it is extremely important to be vigilant and stand firm in your distinctive perspective—be it more optimistic than pessimistic or be it more realistic than opportunistic. Regardless of where your perspective falls on the spectrum, you must fight for it.

The number one reason that you must fight for your perspective is because it uniquely shapes you like a signature, a trademarked logo. Our perspectives represent the brand of who we are. We live in a brand-centric society; everybody is trying to build their brand, and business-minded people are always looking for innovative branding ideas to increase their marketability. So, I raise this question to you: how are you building your brand?

Check out this highlight from the vault of the "brand of Jesus." John 4:1–3 says, *"When Jesus realized that the Pharisees were aware He was gaining and baptizing more disciples than John (although it was not Jesus who baptized but His disciples), He left Judea and returned to Galilee"* (BSB).

Quick Hesitation Dribble

Before we go any further, let's pause to understand the significance of this moment. Jesus baptizing more people than John is like Lebron James passing Kareem Abdul-Jabbar on the NBA's all-time scoring list. It's a massive deal because John baptized so many folks, that everybody just started calling him John "the Baptist" or John "the Baptizer."

Baptizing folks was what John did daily. He was in the business of dipping folks in the water. As a matter of fact, he even baptized Jesus. John the Baptist knew that Jesus, the Messiah, was coming. So, while he waited for the Messiah to come, John became a walking, talking commercial for Him. He would say things like, "You think I'm something, just wait until the Messiah comes. He's going to be much greater than I am. As a matter of fact, I'm not even going to be James-Worthy of lacing this guy's sneakers."

So, John prepared the way for the Messiah, Jesus, to come through mobile advertisement, and he was an essential factor in building the brand of Jesus.

Branding 101

As you build your brand, be aware that your reputation precedes you. Your first encounter with someone is not necessarily their first encounter with you. In most cases, people have either heard of you or profiled you based on an idea of who they believe you are. It's crazy how people will think they know you without getting to know you. Regardless of how messed up this is, just be authentically you. Overcome all prejudicial assumptions and establish your perspective. Build your brand.

As I build my own brand, I envision my signature trademarked logo being the shape of a circle. This is because circles do not take sides; circles are not boxed in. Circles are consistent and perpetual. So, while my ideal perspective takes on a shape that remains objectively subjective, unapologetically bending toward Christ, you must determine the shape of *your* unique perspective and build your own brand (BYOB).

Get That Shot Outta Here

As we make our pitch to establish our brand, we must be aware of the existential power of deflecting. To understand the power of deflecting in its fullness, we need to know that the prefix "de-" means separation, negation, and reversal. The root word *flect* means to bend. Together, the word *deflect* means to reverse one's bend or to negate one's bend.

Deflecting is one of the primary powers that we fight against as we shape our perspective because its main objective is to bend our perspective out of shape:

- This is the power that we find on television (tell-a-vision), where the goal is to tell a vision (the world's vision) and cause us not to focus on the vision (God's vision).
- This is the power that we find on social media (me-to-ya), which we use with the intention to take our focus off "me" and to focus on "ya" instead.
- This is the power that we find in politics (poly-ticks), where we constantly realize that even in our democracy, many laws and philosophies seem to be present just to tick people off.

In the mid '80s and early '90s, two powerful deflecting giants from the great continent of Africa joined in the NBA. In 1984, Nigerian native, Hakeem "The Dream" Olajuwon, entered the NBA as the number one pick after an outstanding college career at the University of Houston. Though Olajuwon is most notable for his offensive dominance and his graceful "dream shaking" finesse, his defensive presence as a shot-blocking nightmare made him the NBA's all-time blocks leader.[37]

Second on the NBA's all-time blocks list is the Congolese native, Dikembe Mutombo, who was a defensive force of nature. He would intimidate his opponents, daring them to drive the ball to the hole and then wag his finger at them after he rejected their shot as to say, "Not in my house!"[38]

As you form your unique perspective of life and shape the purview of your brand, you must properly size up the finger-wagging nightmare of deflectors and be assured that you are always taking your best shot.

Goaltending

The most effective way to get off the shot of your perspective despite prominent deflectors and defenders is by reflecting. Reflecting is pretty much like working on your floater game to get your shot over great defenders or adding a euro-step to your package to get around them.

If you break down the word *reflect*, you will find that it reminds us of our bend. And trust me, when life hits you like an Oklahoma drill, you *need* to be reminded of your bend, which means you need to reflect.

Reflecting reminds us of our shape and helps us to stay focused on our goals in a way that prevents our shots from being deflected. Ultimately, reflecting is a vital resource that prevents

---

[37] "Legends Profile: Hakeem Olajuwon," NBA History, September 13, 2021, https://www.nba.com/news/history-nba-legend-hakeem-olajuwon.
[38] "Dikembe Mutombo," Basketball Hall of Fame, https://www.hoophall.com/hall-of-famers/dikembe-mutombo/.

us from getting bent out of shape. It is extremely important to reflect in order to protect your perspective, because that is where your sphere of influence and scope of responsibility reside. Reflecting—being reminded of your influence and your responsibility—is like commercials that advertise the most critical components of your brand.

Fundamentally Sound

There is a meditative state of reflection that pushes you back to your foundation, the place where you are forced to focus on your fundamental structure and perhaps unlearn some bad habits that may have formed in your efforts to keep pace and remain relevant. For instance, there's no point in throwing a fancy, no-look pass when a simple two-handed chest pass will get the job done.

One of the most fundamentally sound basketball players of all time, and arguably the best power forward to ever play the game is Tim Duncan. In fact, he is even nicknamed "The Big Fundamental."

The thing that stands out about "Timmy D" is the way he went about his work. He wasn't flashy and never wowed you with spectacular dunks, but his efficiency and effectiveness as a five-time NBA champion were simply out of this world. His approach to the game included incredible footwork, great attention to detail, tremendous physicality, and a basketball IQ that would impress the likes of Albert Einstein.

He dominated his era. His domination reflected his attention to detail and was a direct result of his ability to stay focused on the fundamentals of the game during a time when many of his contemporaries became engrossed with the evolving flashiness of the game.

When I think about Tim Duncan, I envision effectiveness and efficiency in its purest form. Can I push it and take this statement a step further? I believe the way that Tim Duncan played basketball embodies the vision that James Naismith had in mind when he created the game. As a matter of fact, I am all for making Tim Duncan the new logo for the NBA.

Focusing and reflecting on the foundation of who you are helps you embody the vision that God created you for. Basically, everything you do is filtered through the foundation of who you are. Calm down. I know that sometimes bad decisions seep through the cracked foundation of your character, but these decisions are more like anomalies than who you really are. This is why there is such a thing in the court of law as a character witness. These are people who represent you to defend your character. You don't have to defend yourself for the last situation you were in where you acted out of character; I got you! I'll represent you . . . LOL.

Tim Duncan, working on the fundamentals of the game, focusing on the basics of life . . . blah, blah, blah. I know this stuff sounds old-fashioned and doesn't come with flashing lights or bells and whistles, but without a solid foundation, everything that you build is guaranteed to come crashing down.

Power Forward

The predicamental plight of inequality in America is a systemic core issue with one major preeminent contributor: a foundation of *lies*. Every rational person in the world who is in touch with their humanity knows that "One nation under God, indivisible, with liberty and justice for all," is simply not true—not who America is.

This country was founded on extreme fundamentalist values that extend privileges to one people group at the expense of others, and there is no equality in that. To build any measure of equality on top of a constitutional construct that should be condemned is a recipe for destruction.

The only way to firmly establish equality in America is to uproot the deeply ingrained beliefs that this country was erroneously founded on. We have to demilitarize the fundamentalist mindset of this country and no longer settle for merely demonizing it. This is the only way to effectively challenge the prejudicial mindset of America and force it to look at its foundation.

It's not enough to just shine a light on the wickedness that we know exists in the world, but we have to neutralize the threat of wickedness by challenging its foundation and going for the heart. The truth of the matter is that the brand of who you are will always stand on the foundation of your heart. So, always go for the heart, knowing that at the heart of the matter is always a matter of the heart. You go for the heart by having intentional, hard (heart) conversations within your true circles of contact.

For too long, we have been busy forming tokenized relationships instead of building true heart connections. We have to remember that real reconciliation and equality will never be about filling stat sheets and checking certain boxes but will forever be about evaluating the conditions of people's hearts. This is why we must constantly self-evaluate the basic structure and core of who we are to ensure that we are foundationally and fundamentally sound.

If only we could keep it as simple as resting our morals on "loving others as ourselves." That's the championship foundation, right there. While you're busy living, continue to evaluate and strengthen the foundation of who you are because the true character of your brand depends on it.

> *Because of God's grace to me, I have laid the foundation like an expert builder. Now others are building on it. But whoever is building on this foundation must be very careful. For no one can lay any foundation other than the one we already have—Jesus Christ. Anyone who builds on that foundation may use a variety of materials—gold, silver, jewels, wood, hay, or straw. But on the judgment day, fire will reveal what kind of work each builder has done. The fire will show if a person's work has any value. If the work survives, that builder will receive a reward. But if the work is burned up, the builder will suffer great loss. The builder will be saved, but like someone barely escaping through a wall of flames.*
>
> —1 Corinthians 3:10–15 NLT

Expanding Your Brand

Let's examine the second highlight from the vault of the "brand of Jesus," which lands us at John 4:2. Remember, verse 2 says, *"although in fact it was not Jesus who baptized, but His disciples."* Now check this out: Jesus's disciples were doing all the baptizing, but Jesus was still getting all the credit. In this, not only was the brand of Jesus built, but His brand was expanded through His disciples.

Everybody knows who Nike is, right? The swoosh and "Just Do It"? Right . . . dem folks. Nike is the most ubiquitous sports brand in the entire world. Nike is popular for their clothing apparel, but even more so for their shoes. There is an appreciation and level of respect that must be given to the brand that Nike has built, and this appreciation intensifies when you consider how they have expanded over the years. Part of this expansion revolves around Nike's signature basketball shoes. They have shoes linked with major superstars including Giannis Antetokounmpo, Kevin Durant, Kyrie Irving, and the king himself—Lebron James. Nike shoes operate as subsidiary, standalone products that fall within the brand of Nike. And guess what? As they sell, the Nike brand still gets credit. Whether you like it or not, as you operate within your sphere of influence, your brand is being expanded.

Endorsement Deal

We have a responsibility to make sure that the product that others sell by partnering with us is something that we want to get credit for. We find this principle in 2 Corinthians 10:15–16 (NIV):

> *Neither do we go beyond our limits by boasting of work done by others. Our hope is that, as your faith continues to grow, our sphere of activity among you will greatly expand, so that we can preach the gospel in the regions beyond you. For we do not want to boast about work already done in someone else's territory.*

The most challenging thing about this passage is that it strongly encourages us to dominate within our sphere of influence as we expand our brand. I'm talking about dominating like Wilt Chamberlain, who went so hard in the paint that the NBA had to change their rules to slow him down.

The words, 'greatly expand,' used together are not playground words, but communicate that it is time to dominate. Now let's go inside of the telestrator like Kenny Smith to take a closer look at the terms and conditions of 2 Corinthians 10:15–16. The passage suggests that as I grow in my faith, I can influence others to carry out their assignments. This means that as my actions, which are based upon the Word of God mature, I begin to dominate within my sphere of influence.

This notion of dominating within my sphere of influence cannot happen unless my faith grows, because only then will I think of others enough to help them become assignment-driven. My only chance at dominating is by valuing the lives of others to the degree that I place a premium on their purpose. The last time I checked, placing a premium on another person's purpose requires self-sacrifice.

Essentially, it is impossible to be others-oriented and self-centered at the same time. The real problem is that being others-oriented is extremely complicated when you have so many unanswered questions about yourself. You must identify your true identity and get to know yourself by spending some quality time with you.

One thing that you learn by looking at the life of Jesus is that He definitely knew who He was. Once we have the foundation of who we are figured out and truly know who we are, then we can grow, build, expand, and dominate.

Quick question: How are you doing within your sphere of influence? Don't answer that question because it wasn't just a quick question; it was also a trick question. And the reality is, it is not ours to answer, because when it comes to our sphere, our effectiveness is generally answered through the lives of the people within it.

Dominating within one's sphere is not for the faint at heart. So, you must not lose heart or get weary in doing well, for you will reap your reward if you don't give up.

Protecting Your Brand

The great Floyd "Money" Mayweather says, "In the end, you have to protect yourself at all times."[39] Proverbs 4:23 says, *"Above all else, guard your heart with all diligence, for everything you do flows from it."* As we establish and expand our brand by impactfully influencing people within our sphere in dominant fashion, we must always protect the heart of it. When dealing with human nature, remember that baggage is included in the equation. In addition, we are human ourselves, so we can easily become the biggest threat to our heart, even more than others. For these reasons, we need protective measures in place, clauses within our contract, and boundary-like parameters that we are not to cross, lest we be whistled out of bounds.

It is critical for us to understand the scope of our responsibility as we live to dominate within our sphere. Our scope of responsibility conveniently lies within our sphere to

---

[39] "Floyd Mayweather Jr. Quotes," accessed July 23, 2020, https://www.brainyquote.com/authors/floyd-mayweather-jr-quotes.

hold us accountable and for our own protection. Not only does it protect us, but it also serves as a preventative measure that lessens the risk of injury. It is imperative that we understand the scope of our responsibility in every relationship. Without this understanding, we unnecessarily blame ourselves for other people's issues. I have seen that happen too many times. You start blaming yourself for other folks' problems, which easily leads to low self-esteem and feeling like a failure, and before you know it, instead of protecting yourself, you're hurting yourself.

I recall one time when a friend was being hard on herself, thinking she did not do enough to help a couple whose relationship was in trouble. She felt this way because she was unable to provide them with the resolution that they desired. I quickly sat her down and said, "Nope, I can't let you beat yourself up over this, especially when you did what you were supposed to do. I know you were expecting a different result and that you wanted to help them more than you could, but you have to understand 1 Corinthians 3:6 in which Paul says, *"I planted, Apollos watered, but God gave the increase"* (KJV).

I told her to notice the rhythm of this verse and how each entity had a distinct responsibility. Paul had a responsibility to plant; Apollos had a responsibility to water, and God had the ultimate responsibility to provide an increase. Paul and Apollos had a responsibility of applying principle and honoring process, but the results did not fall within their scope of responsibility, for that was God's responsibility.

Listen, I get it. It's hard to totally trust God with results, especially when we live in such a results-oriented world. It seems as though the world constantly announces with the booming voice of Michael Buffer, "Successful results are the only thing that matter." Well, I fight back against what the world says about results with a powerful combination of verses found in John 15.

John 15:4 throws the first punch, a right jab, by saying, *"Remain in me, as I also remain in you. No branch can bear fruit by itself; it must remain in the vine. Neither can you bear fruit unless you remain in me."* Then, John 15:5 throws a left hook by saying, *"I am the vine; you are the branches. If you remain in me and I in you, you will bear much fruit; apart from me you can do nothing."* The knockout punch, a right uppercut, is thrown in John 15:8, which says, *"This is to my Father's glory, that you bear much fruit, showing yourselves to be my disciples."*

At first take and second glance, you would believe that this combination of verses is trying to get you, as the branch, to focus on the result of bearing much fruit. But through a "Thrilla in Manila" rematch of the view, you realize that this combination is trying to get us, as branches, to honor the process of staying connected to the vine.

TKO

Success is the result of staying connected to the One who rewards those connected to Him with successful results. As much as we try to serve as judges with scorecards, controlling results, that job just doesn't fall in our wheelhouse. It does not land within our squared circle of responsibility; however, the process of staying connected always does.

We can never become the champions that God has designed us to be until we begin training like champions. This is why we must learn to value processes more than we value results. If we don't, we delay the promises of God from days to decades . . . just ask the Israelites.

Various translations of 2 Corinthians 10:12–13 tell us that we would not dare put ourselves in the same class with, or compare ourselves to, those who recommend themselves. Whenever they measure themselves by their own standards or compare themselves among themselves, they show how foolish they are. We, however, will not deal with things beyond our measure—outside of our scope, but we will stay within the scope of the sphere which God apportioned and appointed to us as a measure, a measure that includes you.

There is one last glowing highlight from the vault of the "brand of Jesus" that I want to show you from Chapter 4 of the Gospel of John, which occurs when Jesus meets a Samaritan woman at Jacob's well. Here are the highlights of the encounter:

> *When a Samaritan woman came to draw water, Jesus said to her, "Will you give me a drink?" (His disciples had gone into the town to buy food.)*
>
> *The Samaritan woman said to him, "You are a Jew, and I am a Samaritan woman. How can you ask me for a drink?" (For Jews do not associate with Samaritans.)*
>
> *Jesus answered her, "If you knew the gift of God and who it is that asks you for a drink, you would have asked him, and he would have given you living water."*
>
> —John 4:7–10

The Samaritan woman was surprised that Jesus was even talking to her because she identified Him as being a Jew, but that wasn't His full identity. It amazes me how people can identify you, labeling you as this or that with absolutely no knowledge of who you truly are. She profiled Jesus, just like we profile people today. But look at Jesus's response and how He adamantly protected His brand. He pretty much said, "You don't really know me, but I can for sure show you who I am. If you knew the gift of God that I am, you would realize that I have way more to offer you than this idea in your head that you have branded me with."

Rumble in the Jungle

I'm super busy protecting my brand against myself, because, trust me, I have made many mistakes to taint my brand. So, I'll be a boxer's uncle if I'm going to allow my brand to be tarnished by people who don't even know me.

The only way to protect your brand is to allow your God-given gifts to rumble free in your spirit. This reminds me that I failed to mention earlier, when talking about my results-minded friend, that I actually gave her a split-decision. While I admonished her for thinking she hadn't done enough, I commended her for wondering if she could have done more. That's Heavyweight Champion DNA right there.

This is what you must know: you are much more than what any social or cultural construct could ever brand you to be. There is, in fact, a greater potential that lies on the inside of you that you haven't even realized yet. It rumbles deep from within the brand of who you are, and it must be drawn out. I don't know about you, but I refuse to settle for anything less than God's best. I refuse to establish a brand that's afraid to venture outside of comfortability—a brand that doesn't strive to reach its full potential in Christ. Now is the time for all the potential that has been lying dormant inside our brand to rumble. So, rumble, young man, rumble.

Check out the final part of this highlight from John 4:

> "Sir," the woman said, "I can see that you are a prophet. Our ancestors worshiped on this mountain, but you Jews claim that the place where we must worship is in Jerusalem."
>
> "Woman," Jesus replied, "believe me, a time is coming when you will worship the Father neither on this mountain nor in Jerusalem. You Samaritans worship what you do not know; we worship what we do know, for salvation is from the Jews. Yet a time is coming and has now come when the true worshipers will worship the Father in the Spirit and in truth, for they are the kind of worshipers the Father seeks. God is spirit, and his worshipers must worship in the Spirit and in truth."
>
> The woman said, "I know that Messiah" (called Christ) "is coming. When he comes, he will explain everything to us."
>
> Then Jesus declared, "I, the one speaking to you—I am he."
>
> —John 4:19–26

Now, to the Samaritan woman's credit, she started warming up to who Jesus was. He went from being just another Jew to being a prophet who was also a Jew. However, she was unable to accurately estimate His full potential, even after He gave her a glimpse of the power within. Before you start judging her, this is our reality because most of the time, we are only able to process others by peeling them back one layer at a time.

"Real Deal" Holyfield

Let's agree that we meet a person's representative before we actually meet them. For this reason, it is important not to allow ourselves to get rope-a-doped by a person's first impression, but instead to peel them back one layer at a time. What's the rush? Who do you think you are . . . Mike Tyson, or something? Quickly going for the knockout punch makes you susceptible to being knocked out.

As people peel back the layers of who you are, pray they don't bite your ear off. Seriously, know that they are going to underestimate your potential. Don't get mad at them because they can never know you as well as you know you.

During this encounter when the woman from Samaria was getting to know Jesus, He doesn't get upset when she underestimates His potential. Instead, He does something that He almost never does. He directly reveals to her who He truly is, the Messiah.

This makes sense and adds up on the scorecard of my mind. Jesus wanted to be understood, just like you and I want to be understood. However, He typically tempered understanding by speaking in parables and revealing Himself in layers so as not to overwhelm feeble human minds. Occasionally, He would hit people with the "I am the Light of the World," or "I am the Bread of Life," or, my favorite, "I am the Way, the Truth and the Life."

Jesus meticulously and methodically set up His punches as He revealed Himself to the world in layers. But, with this woman, He didn't pull any punches. Instead He packed a knockout punch that literally changed her life.

In the early rounds of the conversational bout, He hit her with, *"Anyone who drinks the water that I can give will never thirst—not ever"* (MSG). But eventually, He revealed to her His true, full identity as the Messiah.

Power Punches Landed

For us to have the type of impact that God designed us to have, we must have intentional, isolated, progressive encounters with Christ.

Make no mistake about it; the conversation between Jesus and this woman progressed the way that it did because they were alone. There was no crowd and no posse because Jesus intentionally sent the disciples away. Jesus planned this isolated encounter with the Samaritan woman. He knew that executing a calculated game plan was crucial to creating a moment of impact.

Successful fighters have masterful game plans that create moments of impact to help them win. They know how to attack their opponent and how to counter their opponents because they have studied them. They know how to focus on isolated areas that reveal weaknesses in their opponent that they didn't even know existed in themselves. These fighters know how to protect themselves at all times as they carry out their game plan.

As Jesus proclaimed to the woman that He was the Messiah, He protectively put His gloves up to remind Himself of who He was. There will be times when you will need to remind yourself of who *you* are, especially when you exceed the expectations of others. If you are not careful, you may let merely living up to their preconceived expectations define you.

You could begin to believe an inner dialogue, "Hey, maybe I do need to just shut up and dribble, or catch, or even punch (depending on the sport you play)." You must remember that you can never fully identify who you are by merely living up to the expectations of others.

The Samaritan woman called Jesus a Jew, which was her preconceived expectation, and Jesus said, "Nope, I'm more than that!" Then the woman called Jesus a prophet, which exceeded her expectations, and Jesus said, "Nope, I would be doing you and me a great disservice if I merely exceeded your expectations; I am still more than that . . . I am the Messiah!"

It's not enough to survive low-income housing and under-resourced neighborhoods, to be the first one in your family to finish college and land your dream job. . . . There is *more*. It's not enough to be validated within all your circles and to be affirmed by all your peers—accepted by whites, adored by blacks, appreciated by baby boomers, admired by millennials: "Everybody loves Rickey!" So what? There is still *more*. God's brand is a brand of *more*. Protect your brand by protecting His brand. Jesus protected His brand by knowingly, steadfastly, against all odds, continuing to be **all** that the Father created Him to be, and we must do the same.

Coaching Keys to Victory

As you build your brand, remember to:

- Choose flexibility over rigidity because there will be many facets and phases of life that contribute to the development of your brand.
- Establish your non-negotiables by asking and answering the questions "Who am I?" and "Why am I?" I am _____ because of _____ accurately defines your non-negotiables and protects the foundation of your brand from experiencing cracks as you expand.
- Respect your brand at all times, even when others disrespect it. Ultimately, it doesn't matter what others think as long as you remain true to who you are. After all, you are the poster child for your brand.

POST-GAME INNER-VIEW

I pray that your Most Valuable Possession has identified Christ as the bullseye of your perspective. I pray that your arrow of purpose has been locked and loaded onto your bow of life. This is your season of release, your season of maximized influence. This is your time to break away from the distracted culture of comparison traps, the time to unleash all your unlocked potential. This is the season to shift and transform your mindset into one that is favorable for growth. It's time to process everything that has been incubating within the confines of your secret place. Target acquired. Take a deep breath. Sense the power within as you. Pull. Release. Make your shot!

CHAMPIONSHIP PARADE

A very special thanks goes to my wife, Reagan, who has been extremely supportive throughout this entire process. I don't even want to think about what I would do without you.

To Dad and Gigi, Candice Fondren, Eric Hobbs, Ron Hobbs, Cleo Hobbs, Reginald Hobbs, Bryan and Loye Ellsworth, Cheryl Browne, Ron and Ann Mears, Scott Smith, Adrienne Hughes, Pastors E. J. and Rachel Brown, Ken Taylor, Anthony Smith, Freda Braddock, Allie MacNeil, Darnell Harris, Jacqueline Netters, Michael Olmstead, Chuck Lawson, and countless others, . . . thank you for helping me kickstart this process.

ABOUT THE AUTHOR

Rickey Fondren II was born in Memphis, Tennessee, where he currently resides. Rickey is a graduate of Strayer University, holds a Certificate of Biblical Studies from Memphis City Seminary, and is currently pursuing a Master of Divinity at Memphis City Seminary. He is a pastor at Hope Church Memphis, leading a community for single and young adults called The Collective. Because Rickey loves God first and basketball second, God inspired him to weave the two together in The Playbook to encourage readers to chase after biblical principles as they enjoy basketball stories.

Rickey is married to Reagan, and they have two children.